What's a Hoy?

A Guide To Modern Boating

What's a Hoy?

A Guide To Modern Boating

BY CAP'N DREW BROWN

Illustrated by Cap'n Drew Brown
(It was cheaper that way)

Published by Argo Press
New York

Portions of this originally appeared in Boating on the Hudson Magazine.

This edition first published 2002 by
Argo Press, Inc.
P.O. Box 655
Shrub Oak, NY   10588

Library of Congress Control Number 2002090567

Brown, Andrew J.
        What's A Hoy? A Guide To Modern Boating/ Andrew J. Brown

1. Humor- Anecdotes, facetiae, satire, etc.   2. Boating Humor

Edited by Diane Hitter

ISBN 0-9718540-0-9

Thank you to my wife, Windlass a.k.a. Meg and my children,
Fender and Cleat a.k.a. Jackie and Steven who suffered through
my cursing at the computer every night while I wrote this.
Thanks to Diane, Bob, Denise and Marianne for their support.
A special word of thanks to John Vargo who got me started in this
whole mess.

Special bow to the wit and creativity of the best selling author
Bruce Feirstein *Real Men Don't Eat Quiche*.

Printed in the United States of America

This book is dedicated to the memory of
Sgt. Daniel H. Petithory, U.S. Army Special Forces.
Killed in action, Afghanistan-December 5, 2001.
Defender of Freedom, Hero, Friend.

His honor and his courage were rivaled only by his kindness and
his sense of humor.

He always loved a good laugh.

**A portion of the proceeds of this book will be donated
to the Daniel H. Petithory Scholarship Fund.**

Table of Contents

Top Ten Lists **77**

Reader Letters **89**

Seafaring Recipes **115**

There are people out there who take boating very seriously. Those people wish for everyone to take boating as seriously as they do. There are also people who take marshmallows very seriously. Certainly, if you were to attend a board of directors meeting at a major marshmallow company, you would find many people who consider the making of marshmallows to be quite a grave and important task. However, for the rest of us, marshmallows and boating are simply not solemn topics and should not be taken too seriously.

Cap'n Drew's monthly column *Ask Cap'n Drew* first appeared in Boating On The Hudson Magazine in September 2000. It is an advice column with a humorous twist that addresses questions and concerns not only about boats, but about every aspect of boating. Although the magazine circulates along the Hudson River in New York and New Jersey, letters and e-mail began pouring in from boaters all over the country. Due to the high demand for completely inane and unusable boating advice, Cap'n Drew decided that it was time to share his knowledge with a world audience.

You can contact Cap'n Drew through the publisher or visit his website at
http://www.capndrew.com

Introduction

Years ago, being a boater was much simpler than it is today. In the boating of yesteryear, owning a personal watercraft meant that you didn't have a partner. Drinking beer was encouraged, life vests were optional, and nobody gave a damn about the environment. Boats were made of wood as opposed to the unpronounceable (albeit superior) products used today that have a life span equivalent to that of petrified wood.

Modern boating has become far more complicated. Today's boaters must deal with complexities such as BWI, environment-friendly emissions, luxury tax, maceration laws and courtesy. Gone are the days of hopping on one's boat and cruising off into the sunset without a care. Today's boaters are expected to observe navigation rules, to concern themselves with the safety of children, and pay for gas costing more per gallon than Dom Perignon.

Therefore, this book is not so much about boats as it is about *boating*. Hopefully it will help boaters make more sense out of our little corner of the world.

The History of Boating

It is said that you cannot know the present unless you know the past. This is especially true of boating since the boating industry has been around for millions of years. We hear that prostitution is the second oldest profession in the world. It is a little known fact that boating is the third. While both are equally noble, the boating industry has advanced much further in its complexity. Throughout the ages, boating technology has steadily advanced to the level that we see today. Whether in dugout canoes or jet engine-racing boats humans have always yearned to depart solid ground and hit the high seas, an element for which we are completely unsuited.

History is chock full of people who have spent nearly all of their retirement money on boats. In this respect, people from thousands of years ago are very much the same as the people of today. Whether they were wearing bearskins, loincloths, tunics or bathing suits people have always followed their desire to grab the family and hop on some floating object to get away from it all.

It is for this reason that the first section of this book is dedicated to the founding fathers of boating. It is to these zany, fun loving boaters of antiquity that we owe our wonderful pastime. We must understand them before we can truly understand ourselves.

The Cavemen

Around 30,000 years ago, in the southern part of France there lived a very well to do caveman by the name of Thag or Gak or something along those lines. He was doing quite well for himself by caveman standards. He had several hairy and muscular wives and a large cave with very few rats. Thag had the whole fire thing down pat, and the wolves hadn't carried off any of his children in months.

One bright summer day, Thag bagged himself a rather large mammoth and it occurred to him that he could take the rest of the summer off. He couldn't decide what to do until one day, while walking on the beach he noticed a log floating on the water. Thag, now inspired, proceeded to find his own long, straight log and spent the next two weeks hollowing it out with his axe. This dug-out canoe was the first recreational boat ever made. He then strapped a primitive outboard motor onto the back and a new pastime was born. Thag eventually started the first marina where he gouged the Neanderthals top dollar for slip space (this is now considered to be one of the primary reasons for the extinction of the Neanderthals).

It is widely known that boating was extremely popular with the Ancient Egyptians. Around 5,000 years ago, they began building boats out of papyrus reeds. They also used papyrus to make paper. Archeologists are still completely baffled as to why these people could build 300 foot pyramids, but it took them over 2,000 years to figure out that paper wasn't the best thing to use to build a boat.

At around 2,500 B.C., Pharaoh Cheops figured out that wood might work a little better than paper, so the factories began to manufacture boats from cedar wood that was imported from Lebanon. This created another problem—propulsion. Since wood is considerably heavier than papyrus, the sails they used could not get these new boats up to the same speeds as the old boats. This greatly displeased Pharaoh Cheops (who was known to be an avid water skier). As a result, they turned to the best source of power they knew – slaves. When conquering an enemy army, the Egyptians would routinely enslave the survivors and make them row boats for them. Today, we gauge our engines by "horsepower," back then, boats were measured by "slave-power." One could often overhear the rich folks over at the Cairo Country Club bragging, "Well, Mr. ▰▰▰▰▰▰ , my yacht has a fifty slave power engine, what's yours?"

3

It is also worth mentioning that Ancient Egypt produced the first known naval war hero, Pharaoh Ramses III. In about 1180 B.C., Ramses won the first known naval battle with the "Sea Peoples" (whoever they were) by using his boats to ram theirs. After taking his place in history, he retired and invented Ramses condoms, which are still widely used today.

The ancient Greeks were known for two things: naked Olympics and naked boating. In fact, they were quite fond of doing most things naked. Some scholars think that this was because they were in awe of the human body; others believe that they were just too damn lazy to pull their pants up. Whatever the reason, there were a hell of a lot of indecent people cruising around in the northern Mediterranean back then.

In around 525 B.C. the Phoenicians, who were rivals of the Greeks, introduced a boat called the bireme. This was a war galley that had two levels of oars and a sail. This allowed for both speed and distance and put the Phoenicians on the map as a new sea power. The ancient arms race was on! About twenty-five years later, the Greeks built a three level war galley that was bigger and faster than the bireme. This ship was aptly (if unimaginatively) named the trireme and was considered to be the most advanced war galley of the time.

The trireme reached a maximum size of 120 feet and was commanded by the trierarch who could be found sitting on his lazy, ancient ass in a large seat at the stern. The trireme was rowed by 170 men, 85 on each side with only the topmost level able to actually see the water. This was a low paying job and most of them were ultimately killed in battle, but they were naked and they were on boats so it made it all worthwhile.

The Romans

The most renowned ship of the Roman times was actually the Roman merchant ship. This ship was widely used in the 2nd century A.D. and was about 180 feet long and had a 46-foot beam. It was powered by the wind and had gigantic holds that could carry vast amounts of cargo. It has been called the lifeblood of the Roman Empire as it facilitated most of the commerce that took place between its cities and provinces across the Mediterranean Sea. It was used to transport grain, corn, wine, olive oil, cloth, as well as the wild animals used for fighting contests in the amphitheaters.

Unfortunately, it would also carry more than a few rats. These rats carried the plague and spread it across the Roman Empire from the Middle East in A.D. 166. This was clearly a low point in boating history. It was also a time of major decline in the popularity of rats. After this, they would never again enjoy the esteem that humans once held for them. Even to this day, they are seldom kept as house pets.

The most notable contribution of the Roman merchant ship to the maritime world was the poopdeck. This aptly named section of the ship extended out over the stern of the ship and had a slotted floor so that the sailors could relieve themselves without having to stretch their extremities over the sides of the ship. It is hard to believe that this little invention had been overlooked until this point. It would seem that every time someone crapped all over the side of his own ship, some sort invention to remedy the situation would come to mind. It's a wonder that modern indoor plumbing wasn't invented around this time.

The Norsemen (meaning North Men) were a civilization based in the northern part of Europe just north and west of the Baltic Sea. Contrary to popular belief, they were actually a peaceful and democratic people who thrived for centuries on an agriculture-based economy. They were also traders and explorers whose influence reached as far to the east as Iraq and as far west as the Americas (which would probably today be called the Eriksons if the Vikings had been able to hang on to it). They were superb metal smiths and, most importantly, outstanding shipbuilders. The term Viking refers only to the Norsemen who went out on raids. All Vikings were Norse, but not all Norsemen were actually Vikings. The name Viking probably comes from the Norse word Vik, meaning bay. Therefore, the term Viking can be loosely translated to – "those who cruise around in Bayliners."

Their famed vessel is known as the Viking longship. It ranged in size from 60 to about 160 feet long. It was constructed from overlapping oak planks sealed with wool string that was dipped in tar. These extremely durable vessels were powered both by wind and by rows of oarsmen This enabled them to cross hundreds of miles of unforgiving ocean yet run circles around their enemy's boats in tight quarters. A steering oar was mounted on the rear, right-hand side. This was called the styri, the Norse word for rudder. This is the origin of the modern word "starboard." In addition, the Vikings produced many well-known historical figures such as Erik the Red, Leif Eriksson, and Hagar the Horrible.

The age of the Vikings began in the late 8th century and continued well into the 15th century. During this time, they used these longships to launch terrifying raids on poorly defended coastline villages in Britain, Ireland, and France. Being Scandinavian, most of these Vikings had long blond hair and blue eyes. To the residents of these poor towns, it must have looked like they were being attacked by Bon Jovi.

By about 870 A.D., the Norse grew tired of simply smacking around their European neighbors so they packed up their families and their belongings, hopped into their Bayliners, and set off into the Atlantic. They first landed in Iceland where they settled and established colonies. It wasn't long before they discovered that Iceland was too cold to grow barley, which was necessary to brew beer. As a result, many of them packed up their families in their boats and set back out across the Atlantic to find a more hospitable place to live (were these people boaters, or what?). They shoved off and soon discovered what was essentially a large block of ice in the North Atlantic, which they named Greenland. It is an interesting footnote to history that they named a green, lush island Iceland and a glacier covered island Greenland- they were probably drunk. They colonized Greenland and began lively trading with the indigenous Inuit, whom they referred to as skraeling, a Norse word for wretch or scared weakling (am I the only one who finds this hysterical?). It didn't take very long to realize that they weren't going to grow any beer there, and slapping around Eskimos wasn't even good sport for these hearty people, so they left a settlement, hopped back into their boats and shoved off yet again. They finally bumped into the Americas near Newfoundland. However they decided to call it Vinland meaning wine land (did they have booze on their minds, or is it my imagination?). They never truly settled the Americas. Being beer drinkers, they knew that wine is for sissies. They gradually began moving back east and their civilization eventually divided into kingdoms, which ultimately became Norway, Sweden and Denmark.

The Vikings brought boating out of the dark ages and made the world realize that it was here to stay. Every boater's secret dream is to pull up to an island and start beating the hell out of its defenseless inhabitants. Although this is no longer socially acceptable, the Vikings ensured that it would stay in the world's collective memory, thereby giving boaters an elevated level of respect for centuries to come.

Some words that almost rhyme with
Norseman

1. Oarsman

2. Lost man

3. Bored man

4. Of course, man

5. Dorsal

6. Boss Man

7. Divorced man

8. Horseman

Famous Moments

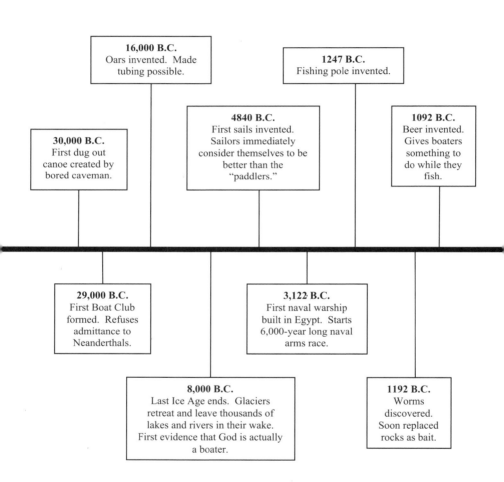

16,000 B.C.
Oars invented. Made tubing possible.

1247 B.C.
Fishing pole invented.

4840 B.C.
First sails invented. Sailors immediately consider themselves to be better than the "paddlers."

1092 B.C.
Beer invented. Gives boaters something to do while they fish.

30,000 B.C.
First dug out canoe created by bored caveman.

29,000 B.C.
First Boat Club formed. Refuses admittance to Neanderthals.

3,122 B.C.
First naval warship built in Egypt. Starts 6,000-year long naval arms race.

8,000 B.C.
Last Ice Age ends. Glaciers retreat and leave thousands of lakes and rivers in their wake. First evidence that God is actually a boater.

1192 B.C.
Worms discovered. Soon replaced rocks as bait.

In Boating History

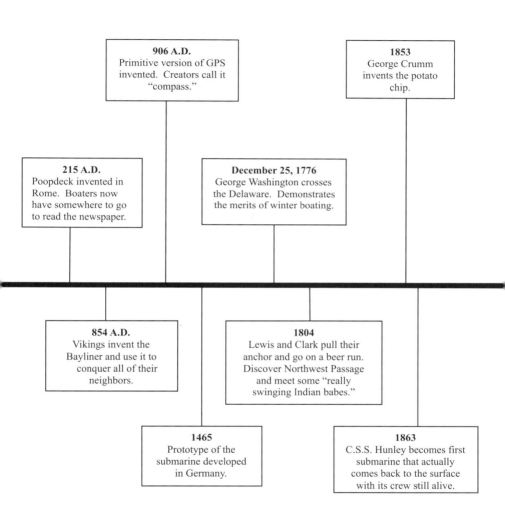

906 A.D.
Primitive version of GPS
invented. Creators call it
"compass."

1853
George Crumm
invents the potato
chip.

215 A.D.
Poopdeck invented in
Rome. Boaters now
have somewhere to go
to read the newspaper.

December 25, 1776
George Washington crosses
the Delaware. Demonstrates
the merits of winter boating.

854 A.D.
Vikings invent the
Bayliner and use it to
conquer all of their
neighbors.

1804
Lewis and Clark pull their
anchor and go on a beer run.
Discover Northwest Passage
and meet some "really
swinging Indian babes."

1465
Prototype of the
submarine developed
in Germany.

1863
C.S.S. Hunley becomes first
submarine that actually
comes back to the surface
with its crew still alive.

Famous Moments in Boating History (cont.)

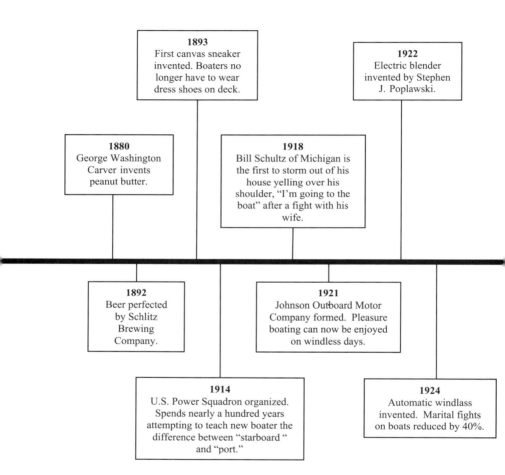

1893
First canvas sneaker invented. Boaters no longer have to wear dress shoes on deck.

1922
Electric blender invented by Stephen J. Poplawski.

1880
George Washington Carver invents peanut butter.

1918
Bill Schultz of Michigan is the first to storm out of his house yelling over his shoulder, "I'm going to the boat" after a fight with his wife.

1892
Beer perfected by Schlitz Brewing Company.

1921
Johnson Outboard Motor Company formed. Pleasure boating can now be enjoyed on windless days.

1914
U.S. Power Squadron organized. Spends nearly a hundred years attempting to teach new boater the difference between "starboard " and "port."

1924
Automatic windlass invented. Marital fights on boats reduced by 40%.

Famous Moments in Boating History (cont.)

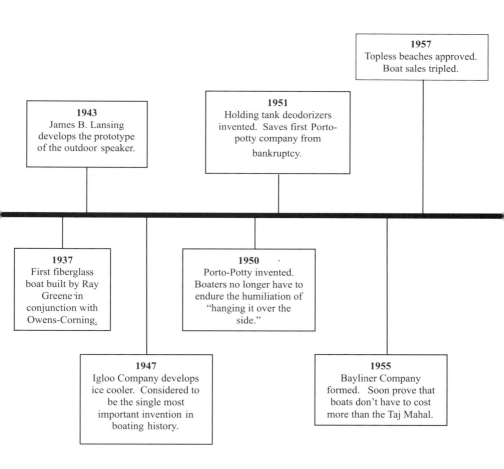

1957
Topless beaches approved.
Boat sales tripled.

1943
James B. Lansing
develops the prototype
of the outdoor speaker.

1951
Holding tank deodorizers
invented. Saves first Porto-
potty company from
bankruptcy.

1937
First fiberglass
boat built by Ray
Greene in
conjunction with
Owens-Corning.

1950
Porto-Potty invented.
Boaters no longer have to
endure the humiliation of
"hanging it over the
side."

1947
Igloo Company develops
ice cooler. Considered to
be the single most
important invention in
boating history.

1955
Bayliner Company
formed. Soon prove that
boats don't have to cost
more than the Taj Mahal.

Famous Moments in Boating History (cont.)

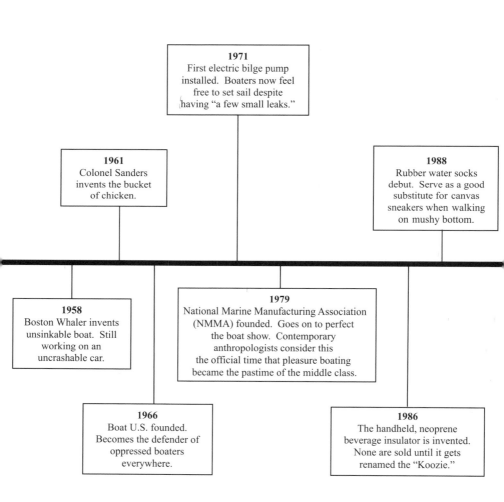

1971
First electric bilge pump installed. Boaters now feel free to set sail despite having "a few small leaks."

1961
Colonel Sanders invents the bucket of chicken.

1988
Rubber water socks debut. Serve as a good substitute for canvas sneakers when walking on mushy bottom.

1958
Boston Whaler invents unsinkable boat. Still working on an uncrashable car.

1979
National Marine Manufacturing Association (NMMA) founded. Goes on to perfect the boat show. Contemporary anthropologists consider this the official time that pleasure boating became the pastime of the middle class.

1966
Boat U.S. founded. Becomes the defender of oppressed boaters everywhere.

1986
The handheld, neoprene beverage insulator is invented. None are sold until it gets renamed the "Koozie."

"I can't believe that you have
twelve pictures of your boat in your wallet,
and not a single one of me."

The Boating Handbook

Do you remember the day that you made the decision to buy your first boat? It was a glorious time of excitement and innocence.   There were a few extra dollars in the bank account; you had some time on your hands and the future looked good.   It was clearly time to start a new hobby, but which one? You never found waiting on line to chase a little ball around a golf course to be very exciting. Besides, the thought of wearing plaid knickers gives you a shiver whenever it comes to mind. You considered collecting stamps, but the doctor warned that all the excitement might not be good for your heart. Everybody knows that bird watching is something you do while you're doing something else. What to do, what to do?

Well, you bought a boat. You always knew that you would someday. Never again would you stand on shore and gaze longingly at all the boaters cruising past you with smiles on their faces, apparently without a trouble in the world. No longer would you cross a bridge and wonder what it would be like to be the person in the boat down below. The thrill gripped your chest like an invisible hand. You were going to become one of them. You enjoyed shopping around and looking at different models. You couldn't possibly tire of talking about boats with anyone who would listen. You secretly enjoyed the idea that they might envy you for having all this disposable cash. It was a dream come true.

In the beginning, you would try to maneuver the words

"my boat" into every conversation. You couldn't wash your new boat enough. Painting it brought you unimaginable joy and you could even spend forty-five minutes changing the oil without ever losing the smile on your face. After all, it takes weeks of changing your new baby's diaper before you actually realize what it is that you're handling.

Then came the end of the innocence. No one had ever mentioned that you needed a P.h.D. in mechanical engineering to fix the motor. How about the first time you noticed that green stuff growing around the water line or when you spent three hours slung over the motor trying to get that last bolt out of a dead starter? How many times did you drop the boat in the water without putting in the plug? Remember that first tow home? Remember the second, third and fourth? What about all those "boat bruises" that appeared on your arms and legs after a long day out on the water? You soon came to realize that there was more to boating than the wind in your hair and the spray on your face.

But you never got (completely) discouraged and momma didn't raise any quitters. There are millions of boaters out there; they can't all be going through this, right? It began to seem that you were the only one with all the problems. Everyone else simply turned the key and went. It took two full seasons for you to realize that the true badge of an "expert" boater is not seamanship but showmanship - the art of making boats look easy and problem free. When was the last time you heard one golfer say to another, "I can't play this game worth a damn. Whoever invented it was a sadist!"? Never. After all, the more you bad-mouth something, the harder it is to explain your addiction to it.

Eventually, everything became easier. The learning curve in boating looks like the Hoover Dam, but it can be mastered. New boaters have to learn seamanship, mechanics, navigation, etiquette, and a whole new language. This is no mean trick considering most boating seasons last only seven months. But remember, in your boating career, most of your bent props occur during the first year (very much like sex in marriage) and, like marriage, if you can make it through the first year, you're home free....

Anyway, we're glad you stuck with it. Without you around, there would be nobody to buy books with lots of boat stuff in them. To use a quote from Kenneth Grahame in *The Wind in the Willows,* "Believe me, my young friend, there is nothing-absolutely nothing- half so much worth doing as simply messing about in boats."

Now that you've survived, there's only one thing that you can do – upgrade.

TOP TEN

Reasons to Buy a Boat:

1. Financial Consultant advised you that hemorrhaging a fortune into a depreciating asset was a sound financial strategy.

2. You want to become intimately acquainted with every single working part of an engine.

3. You find constant scraping, painting and waxing to be very therapeutic.

4. You feel a moral obligation to help support OPEC.

5. Instead of sitting on shore not catching any fish, you prefer to sit on a boat, not catching any fish.

6. You want complete strangers to call you, "Captain."

7. If you drink all day in a bar, you are a "lush." If you drink all day on a boat, you are "enjoying life to it's fullest potential."

8. Aren't some of those knots really cool?

9. You enjoy using a toilet the size of a saucepan.

10. A million Skippers can't be wrong.

Buying a Boat

Buying a boat can be the happiest time in a person's life. The excitement that wells up inside you when shopping for a boat is comparable to the feelings of the bride and groom on the morning of their wedding. It is a feeling of exuberance, love, excitement and possibly hangover. As in marriage, the boat buyer takes on a partner in life. However, unlike a spouse, a boat can be sold when you want to upgrade. Although this can be a great comfort, the potential boat buyer must still take great care in choosing the right boat. It is for this reason that I have assembled a list of frequently asked questions to be carefully considered before buying a boat.

1. **How much should I spend?** This is a commonly asked question with a completely obvious answer. Spend as much as you possibly can. If you don't, you will not be achieving your maximum potential. When shopping for your dream house, would you buy a house with two bedrooms for your six kids if you could afford one with more bedrooms? Absolutely not! Why then would you settle for any less for yourself? Spend until it hurts. If you don't, you will never be a true boater.

2. **What kind of boat should I get?** This can be determined by exercising a little common sense. If you want to water ski, buying a sailboat probably wouldn't be advisable. If entertaining is your thing, rowboats are out (although watching your in-laws wobbling about in a 9-foot dingy can really be quite amusing). If your goal is fishing, you might run into some pretty obvious problems on a jet ski. If you're into speed and performance, keep in mind that pontoon boats seldom win poker runs. Try to find a boat that is suitable for your needs, but if you still can't make up your mind, get one that looks good. Looking good is an extremely important yet very underrated aspect of boat buying. What's the point of boating if you can't look good doing it? Before purchasing a boat, potential buyers should always see how they look on every angle of it. After all, a boat can be completely functional, but who is ever going to buy it if it looks like a big, floating turnip?

3. **How big a boat should I buy?** Get a boat that is as big as possible. Why jerk around? If you buy a boat that is any smaller than you can afford, you're just going to want to upgrade in a year anyway. Save yourself the trouble right at the beginning and you might last a full three years before you consider re-mortgaging your house to buy a larger boat. It's a fact that people with big boats get far more respect than those with smaller ones. The world of boating is very phallic. It also has well-defined social strata that must be adhered to. You will rarely see owners of large yachts socializing on small runabouts. This is a law of nature which defines us as humans. Therefore, it is extremely important for you to start as high on the marine food chain as you can.

4. **How big a motor should it have?** It should have two, possibly three engines and they should be as large as can fit in the boat. If there is any room alongside the motor, you have bought too small a motor. Don't worry about being able to access anything on the engine, that's what marine mechanics are for. Marine mechanics thrive on the challenge. Don't worry about all of the details; if you get too wound up in the minutia of it you will drive yourself crazy.

5. **Where should I buy it?** You have several choices. If you are looking for a used boat, you can find ads in the paper, check for posting at a local marina, or simply ask around. If you are looking for a new boat, you can visit a local dealer or attend the nearest boat show. If you wish to purchase it at a local dealer, you might consider having a private investigator follow the broker around for a few days to determine whether the broker is faithful to his or her spouse. If any hanky panky is discovered, the photos that you obtain can be extremely helpful in the price negotiations. The savings will more than pay the fees charged by the private investigator. This probably will not be an option at the boat show, however, since it typically lasts only a few days. Therefore you must prepare yourself in other ways. People have employed the use of screaming, kicking and even crying to settle at the right price for a boat. One clever boater even went so far as to step in dog poop just before the boat show and hung around all day at the display that held the boat that he wished to purchase. He looked and haggled and milled around until the show closed for the day- driving off every other potential buyer because of the disgusting smell that emanated from his feet. He did this for two days and poor brokers were unable to sell even

one boat. By the third day they were willing to sell him his boat at the wholesale price (they even threw it right on the back of a trailer and took it to his home just to get rid of him). While this may seem a little radical, it proves that there is no extreme that some boaters won't employ to buy the boat they want.

A word about boat shows...

The boat show is an enchanted wonderland at which we revert back to our childhood days of walking endlessly through toy stores, never tiring of looking at row upon row of plastic junk. It is a magic place where anyone can acquire a large yacht by simply signing a piece of paper, regardless of whether the buyer has a job or any other means of paying for it.

The boat show can make you lose your inhibitions to a far greater degree than even the finest scotch. I must confess that a number of years ago, I became so overwhelmed and engrossed at a boat show that I actually began skipping. This can prove quite dangerous, however, as the boat show salesmen take this as a sure sign of weakness. I have overheard these boat brokers bragging to one another about the speed at which they were able to get a "skipper" to sign (it was then that I realized that "skipper" did not mean "Captain").

If you attend a show this year, remember to look up into the rafters. You will see dark suited men in sunglasses whispering into walkie-talkies such things as, "skipper in aisle 2'" or "the guy in aisle 5 is holding a pen."

Things you won't hear at the Boat Show

1. "It's free"

2. "This one here is known as the Yugo of boats."

3. "Sure, hop on. Feel free to push all of the buttons."

4. "Sir, perhaps you should look at something a little less expensive. We wouldn't want you to over-extend yourself."

5. "How the hell should I know how the jet ski turns? I only sell 'em. You'd never actually catch me on the back of one of these suicide-sleds."

6. "Of course it's uncomfortable, Sir. ALL boat beds are uncomfortable."

7. "Don't sign anything now. Why don't you go home and discuss it with your wife?"

8. "Why don't you have your kids hop up and have a look at it?"

9. "Sir, after seeing you and your wife, I'd like to recommend the trim-tab option."

10. "The truth is – they ALL break down constantly."

11. "If you're buying a boat hoping to get yourself a date, trust me, you haven't got enough money."

12. "This little honey was named 'Boat of the Year' by The National Boat-Towing Association."

13. "Actually, they depreciate very rapidly. The reason that they're marked so high is so that I can get my commission."

14. "I once saw a kid bounce out of one of these and fly a full sixty feet."

15. "Sure it's ugly, but so was the Mayflower."

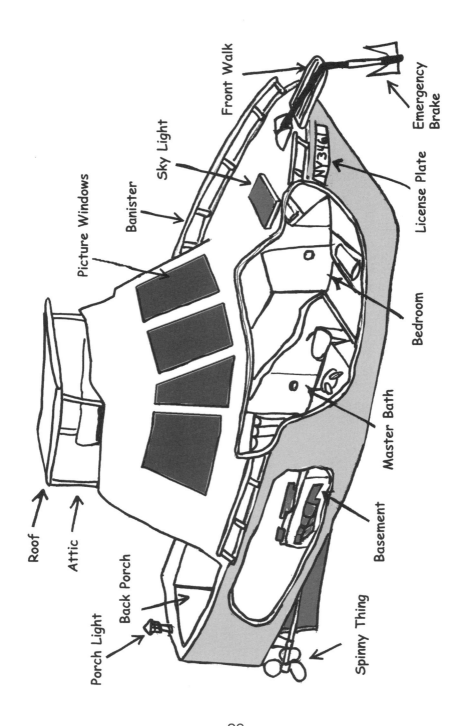

Roof

Attic

Porch Light

Back Porch

Spinny Thing

Basement

Master Bath

Bedroom

License Plate

Emergency Brake

Front Walk

Sky Light

Banister

Picture Windows

Naming a boat is as personal a thing as anyone will ever do. It is like naming a child, only far more difficult. Every boater wants his or her boat to have a completely unique name, but nobody cares if the kid down the street has the same name as your kid. In addition, a boat name has to be witty, clever, and short. They also can tell you quite a bit about the owner. A seasoned boater can tell more about another boat owner by boat name than by a full-scale background check.

Some Boat Names and What They Can Tell You About the Owner

Free Time   I have a strong need to get away from my nagging wife and our horrible, screaming kids

Happy Hours   I have a severe drinking problem and feel a need to share that fact with you

After Taxes   I am a single accountant who doesn't get laid a lot. I'm hoping that this will send a signal that I generate an above-average income

My Toy   It's the only one I have that's more than two inches long

Gypsea   I wanted to combine a common maritime witticism and my latent hatred of indigent, European nomads into a cute boat name

Arbitration   Same as After Taxes but I'm a lawyer

Predator

I have been relentlessly teased and beaten my whole life and now give tough names to everything I own

Inheritance

Hey girls, there might be more...

Summer Wind

Although I try to project a Frank Sinatra image, I am frequently beaten by my lazy, jobless wife

Second Mortgage

Leveraged to the hilt and damned proud of it

Girl Toy

Not quite

Wet Dreams

I am surely wearing a tank top and probably have fuzzy dice on the throttle and carpet on the dashboard

Sea Cow

You should see my wife

College Fund   It's true, I spent it

Stress Buster   I have a massive bleeding ulcer and think
that this might help

Seaducer   Although it doesn't help me get the ladies
one bit, this boat still does wonders for my
self-esteem

Spoiled Rotten   I have a high maintenance wife who isn't
smart enough to get the meaning of this
name. She's a bitch, but the joke is on her

Worst Names for a Boat

1. Stinkpot II
2. Colander
3. Scotch-Breath
4. Mayday
5. Braille Aggressor
6. Moby Slug
7. Dock Urchin
8. Unsinkable
9. Madeline Albright
10. Screw The Coast Guard
11. Lead Bottom
12. Sea Pig
13. The Drip
14. No Vests
15. Tempting Fate
16. Contraband
17. Oil Fire
18. Viagra Falls
19. Can't Happen To Me

Are You A Real Boater?
Boating Quiz #1:

Have You Ever...

1. Fallen off your boat

2. Fallen off a dock

3. Been rocked off a porto-potty

4. Forgotten to put the plug in

5. Spun a prop

6. Taken off with the anchor down

7. Gotten lost on the water

8. Run out of gas

9. Gotten stuck on a sand bar

10. Let your car stay broken so you could spend money to have your boat fixed

11. Paid too much for a boat

12. Not been able to put together a part that you disassembled to fix

13. Been stuck in the rain

14. Dropped a watch or piece of jewelry overboard

Scoring: If you have said yes to 10 or more- you are a REAL boater. 7-10- First Mate. 4-6 Cabin Boy. 0-3 Swabbie.

There comes a moment of decision in every boater's life - whether to trailer the boat or keep it in a marina. Each of these has its good points and bad, but if you decide that the marina life is right for you, you will have to choose one. Unless you are an Eskimo, there are probably a lot of people boating in the same water as you. This means that there will be several marinas in the area. Deciding which marina to join can be a lot tougher than you might think. Be careful to choose wisely or you might wind up stuck in the marina from hell.

How to start? Make a list of all of the marinas within the range that you are willing to travel. If you're lucky, one of them will be owned by your brother-in- law or perhaps by someone of whom you know a deep dark secret. You will probably not be so lucky, however, and will have to shop around using more traditional methods. The most popular method is the "rule out" method. This, of course, is where you scratch off names from your list when they don't meet your criteria. As the list gets smaller, you will be left with only the marinas that make the cut, thus making your decision easier.

Here are a few good reasons to rule out a specific marina:

1. The owner walks through the marina each morning with a Geiger counter

2. You can see more than two thirds of your keel at low tide

3. The nun buoys are real nuns

4. The entire staff of the marina has a total of six teeth

5. The owner has felony level assault charges pending against him

6. The breakwater consists of dead farm animals

7. The dock spiders are bigger than your fist

8. You notice a peculiar stretch of PVC pipe that runs from the pump out station to the snack bar

9. The marina had more than two deaths in the past year that have been attributed to poisonous snakebites

10. They encourage you to blow your bilge water to help dilute the pollution

11. The water rats are associate members

12. The seagulls glow in the dark

13. They share space with the local sewage treatment plant

14. Shore power consists of two live wires hanging off of the end of the dock

15. The dock boys are out on work release

16. The only restroom is an outhouse- and nobody cares

Remember that you will be spending a good deal of time at the marina. It will become your "home away from home." Therefore, you should not make any hasty decisions when choosing one. You should first learn their price structure. If you are prone to fainting, then you might consider calling first, as the prices at some boatyards could throw Bill Gates into shock. Once you know how much each one costs, you can begin to decide what concessions you are willing to make to save money. For example, while some of the more expensive marinas have swimming pools, mine has a swamp. As a result, I was able to greatly reduce my costs. It's a little messy, but it's really not so bad once you get used to the leeches. Besides, I've discovered that the human body can actually develop immunity to several strains of malaria.

It is not always easy to learn everything about a boatyard by simply visiting it a few times. The first marina I joined appeared to have the friendliest people I had ever met. Then I discovered that they all belonged to some network marketing company. The first day I was walking to my boat they trounced me like a bunch of lions on a three-legged zebra. My wife and I made it to our boat and took off, but they chased us for three hours before we finally got away. The next place we joined was built right over an ancient Indian burial ground. I was constantly getting smashed in the face by outdrives as they floated through the air. After that, I stayed in a marina owned by a guy with a chronic case of herring breath. He also had only one eye-which wouldn't have been a problem if he wasn't always scratching it with his pocketknife.

Another area of consideration is the quality of the ship's store. Most marinas have a very convenient store that offers a wide array of supplies and boating necessities. It should be noted that these stores typically operate at a profit margin that makes the Pentagon's four hundred dollar toilet seats look like a magnificent bargain. The benefit is that they are generally open all weekend and they ordinarily carry any parts that you would need. It is arguably better to buy a gas filter that costs more than a small Hyundai than to wait until Monday and lose an entire weekend of boating.

Perhaps the most important factor in the decision making process is the skill of the resident marine mechanic. Some marinas have been known to hire lawnmower mechanics who are only one step ahead of a very serious lawnmower malpractice suit. I learned this while at my fourth boat basin where every time a boat wasn't running smoothly, the mechanic would immediately blame it on the tires. The first time I heard him say this I shot him a puzzled look, to which he replied, "Then you fix it if you're so smart."

Above all take your time when deciding on which marina to use. Be sure to ask a lot of questions and speak to the current members if you can. Whenever possible, do a background investigation and obtain satellite photos. Remember, you can't be too careful!

Good Marina Slogans

1. We May Be Expensive, But We're Expensive

2. Grabbing You By The Balls Since 1968

3. Home of the Indentured Servant

4. There Are No Bad Boats, Just High- Paying Customers

5. Rookie Boaters Are Our Best Clients

6. The Knights of Planned Obsolescence

7. The Gateway to Poverty

8. Home of the Tetanus Tide

9. Hey, At Least We're Close

10. We're Still Cheaper Than a Divorce

11. You Just Keep Coming Back

The Marina Owner

Marina owners are unique among nature's creatures. Typically, they have been brought up on and around boats and been in the boating industry for many generations. This characteristic makes them very much like undertakers and, like undertakers, they can potentially bury you. It also makes them very boring in non boating-related situations.

How to spot the owner of the marina:

1. His leathery skin makes the Marlboro Man look like the Ivory Girl.
2. He's the guy who charges you for directions.
3. He's got fists the size of canned hams.
4. His boat has been on dry dock for years.
5. When his wallet opens, you hear a faint, "cha-ching."
6. He even squints in caves.
7. He wore "chinos" to his daughters wedding.
8. Even his callouses have callouses.
9. You could build a dam with the dirt under his nails.
10. His cologne is "bilgewater musk."
11. His shirt is seven years older than his Cadillac.

"Don't worry kid. I've been fixing
marine engines for years, and there are always
pieces left over when you're done."

Boating Tools

Having the right set of tools is essential to every boater. Being prepared for all contingencies is something an experienced boater takes very seriously. All too often boaters find themselves in trouble and don't have the necessary tools to rectify the problem. A well-equipped toolbox should have everything that a boater might need to be prepared for every possible emergency.

A complete tool kit should include:

1. Adjustable wrench
2. Bottle opener
3. Shot Glasses
4. Swiss Army Knife
5. Corkscrew
6. Condoms
7. Peanut Butter
8. Phone Number of Marine Mechanic
9. Lemons
10. Boat U.S. Membership Card
11. Stirrers
12. Corn Holders

Marine Electronics

Marine Electronics is an extremely important element of modern boating. Since boaters cannot impress other boaters simply by owning a boat, they must acquire as many expensive electronic components as possible to become the envy of their peers. By owning the most advanced electronics, they prove that they are the best and most highly skilled boaters in the group.

Top 10 Electronic Components That No Boat Should Be Without:

1. VHF Radio
2. Depth Finder
3. Blender
4. Ice Maker
5. CD Player
6. Mood Lighting
7. Deep Fryer
8. Air Conditioner
9. Back Massager
10. Automatic Bar

The Boating Life

Have you ever gone to tremendous lengths to plan an absolutely perfect day out on the boat? Did anything work out as planned, anything at all? Don't worry you are not alone. The boating life is a series of adventures and real adventures can't be planned. Planning a perfect day of boating is useless. Experienced boaters call this phenomenon "boat shit" meaning something always goes wrong. A very experienced boater once said," show me someone who has had a perfect day and I'll show you a liar."

Don't fret about it. It is all part of the experience. Believe it or not, the most memorable adventures occur as a result of breakdowns and groundings. Some of the funniest boating stories told are of hapless skippers slung over an engine while his guests wait on the dock and his wife yells at him. While none of this is any fun while we experience it, they become the most vivid memories in the off-season.

46

Boating Ads vs. Boating Reality

Boating Ad	Boating Reality
1. Three beautiful women wearing bikinis are lounging around on deck catching the sun's rays.	1. Your three screaming kids, wearing one water-wing each, are dripping peanut butter and jelly sandwiches all over the deck.
2. Boat drifting serenely in crystal clear, Caribbean-like water	2. Boat rocking violently in murky, highly trafficked water. Pink hospital bag is floating by...
3. Three handsome men on the stern of a forty-foot sport fisherman cruiser holding up what might very well be a record-size tuna.	3. Three drunken slobs tripping over tackle boxes and coolers on a 16-foot outboard with one barely legal bass and a dead battery.
4. Little girl smiling contentedly on a fishing boat with her grandfather (who is also smiling). Sun is up, fish are biting. Caption reads something like, "Take me fishing because soon I'll be grown up."	4. Grandfather is attempting to unravel sixth snarl in reels so far that morning. Transom is so covered in blood and guts of baitfish that it appears an axe murder recently took place there. Little girl sits with elbows on her knees, her ashen face in her hands. The expression on her face reads, "Take me home, because if you don't, I'll continue to vomit with spastic convulsions all over your upholstery."

Boating Ads   VS.   Boating Reality Continued

Boating Ad

5. Boat deliberately grounded in two feet of water on a beautiful, empty beach. Family frolics about in a carefree manner. Picnic blanket spread out slightly above wet sand line bearing various delicacies from four continents.

6. Boat cruising at high speed, on plane, leaving a perfectly symmetrical wake. Everyone on board is smiling- either at each other or off into the distance.

7. Late afternoon and the family is on dock, packing it in after long, but leisurely day on the boat. Boat is pristine. Family looks content and well rested.

Boating Reality

5. Boat unintentionally grounded on a desolate, almost scary beach. Tide has receded to the point where the entire boat is dry and is lying on its side. Father is checking tide charts to determine whether it will be five or six hours before the water will be deep enough for the boat to take float. Mother is sitting on an old towel slightly above the wet sand line desperately trying to remove a piece of glass from the oldest child's foot before the child bleeds to death.

6. Boat is being towed home by towing service. Boat owner is taking up a collection to pay the hefty charge. The only one smiling is the tow guy.

7. Children on dock screaming in pain because of blistering sunburn. Mother is on cell phone with pediatrician to determine whether children should be brought to emergency room. Boat has soda and beer cans strewn about. Jelly is everywhere. Father is attempting to simultaneously secure the boat and apply burn cream to the back of a writhing three year old.

Boating Ads   VS. Boating Reality Continued

Boating Ad

Boating Reality

8. Several couples are sitting quietly on the deck of a boat sipping wine and nibbling on caviar and onions waiting for the entrée of pheasant under glass.

8. Couples are squashed tightly together ravenously shoving pretzels down their throats because the bucket of chicken went over the side after the boat hit that last wake. Everyone is drinking beer from cans, which, upon completion, are thrown into a smelly basket in the stern.

9. Aerial shot of a beautiful, brand new, white cruiser racing across calm water. On deck is a couple who are in their twenties or early thirties. The handsome man at the wheel is wearing a light colored golf shirt stretched tightly over his rippling muscles. Gorgeous woman is wearing seductive bikini. She appears to have just been let out of aerobics prison on work release. Both are tanned to a perfect bronze and their hair flows freely behind them from the wind in their faces. They appear to be ready at any moment to spontaneously rush down below deck and mate wildly like rodents in the springtime.

9. A new, white cruiser race across the water but the couple aboard is rapidly approaching middle age. It has taken until this stage of life to be able to afford anything this expensive. The man at the wheel has a pendulous belly that obscures the little white string that barely secures his bathing suit. This is the result of years of relentlessly drinking vast amounts of beer and eating too many cows. His comb-over flaps behind him like a windsock. The woman is packed into a one-piece bathing suit and strongly resembles a sausage that is wrapped too tight. The vibration of the boat makes her ass-cheeks dance like two squirrels fighting in a bag. Their sex life has obviously been on sabbatical for quite some time- for ergonomic reasons if nothing else...

TOP TEN
Boating Movies

1. The Good, The Bad, and the Out of Gas

2. A Perfect Storm- Followed by a Few Days of Drizzle

3. Dr. Jekyll and Mr. I Can't Get My Damned Friends to Kick In any #@!*&% Money For Gas

4. Clear and Present Shimmy

5. So I Married a Sailboater

6. The Boat Mechanic Who Shagged Me (but good).

7. Scent of a Backfire

8. Three Men and a Failing Boat Partnership

9. When Harry Met the Coast Guard

10. Sunk in Sixty Seconds

Boaters are all too familiar with those strange contusions that appear everywhere on your body after a long day on the water. They are known as boat bruises. Regardless of how calm the water or how relaxing the day, by the time you arrive home there will inevitably be a wide variety of bumps and bruises scattered across your body. These bruises come in every imaginable shape and size, but they all have one thing in common – you don't remember when the hell you got them. This is as deep a mystery in the boating world as the Bermuda Triangle. There is some sort of diminished memory capability that comes with the pastime of boating. It prevents a boater from even vaguely remembering where or at what time he received a compound fracture of his tibia.

There has been much speculation as to the causes of these bruises as well as the reasons why nobody can ever remember getting them. One theory is that boaters are so entranced with their hobby that the mind can involuntarily reduce the speed or totally eliminate the synapses that occur in the nerve endings to notify the conscious mind of pain. The other theory is gremlins. Many boaters believe that little gremlins inhabit all boats and wait for boaters to become excited or otherwise preoccupied then sneak up and whack them about the body with little mallets. Nobody ever sees these creatures but, much like being in a car accident, they will feel the pain at a later time.

I personally credit these bruises to drunkenness on wobbly platforms.

Boating Quiz #2

What do you put down when you need it and pick up when you don't?

Sailboats vs. Powerboats

I am often asked who are the better boaters – power boaters or sail boaters. As much as I hate to admit it, sailors are typically more skilled at boating than power boaters. They must know how the winds and the tides work together. They have to learn which sails to use, and when. They truly have to harness the forces of nature to propel themselves through the water in an adept manner. This gives them a thrill that is a mystery to power boaters. Therefore, as with all things we don't understand, we must treat them with fear and ridicule.

While the advent of the powerboat has diminished the number of sail boaters on the water, there are still many of them among us today. However, keep in mind that it is now widely accepted in anthropological circles that our ancestors actually lived peacefully alongside the Neanderthals for almost 100,000 years before getting so sick and tired of them that they finally decided to kill them off.

"I knew that it was going
to come down to this."

Boats essentially do two things; float and burn gas. Unless you plan on doing nothing but sit on your boat while it's tied to the dock, you will most assuredly be using quite a bit of gasoline during the boating season. Considering the price of gas on the water, this can prove to be quite an expensive venture.

No matter where you go boating or what kind of boat you have, you will probably have guests with you when you go out. The seasoned boater knows how to coerce each and every passenger into sharing the cost of gasoline. This is an acquired skill that involves much tact and sensitivity. No Captain wants to completely offend guests. But no Captain wants to get stuck footing a hefty gas bill to haul guests all over various large bodies of water.

Tips to get guests
to help pay for gas

1. Drop anchor outside a gas dock, and just sit there staring at the pump, sighing wistfully.

2. Trick them into sitting on a "whoopee cushion" then say something like, "well, at least someone has gas."

3. Leave a photo album full of old gas receipts in the head.

4. Hand them an oar and tell them that when gas prices come down you'll start using the motor again.

5. When serving lunch, hand them a plate of beans saying, "This should give you some gas, why don't you reach into your wallet and help me get some?"

6. Tell them that you pledged your children as collateral for the last tank of gas that you bought.

7. Rifle through their wallets while they're swimming.

8. Before you go out, say to them, "I'll bring the donuts if you buy the gas."

9. Siphon gas from their car while they're getting on the boat.

10. Fill the tank then pull the old, "Oops, I left my wallet at home."

11. Have a friend tell them a story about the "Postal Boater" who peppered all of his guests after they refused to pay for gas.

12. Tell them that you don't need to fill the tank. You have the whole next week off and don't care if you drift 'til Wednesday.

The Hackell family planned a wonderful day of boating for a typical Saturday in August. The Hackells are in every way a normal family of five. Mary and Bill Hackell are middle class people who work very hard, take a nice vacation each year and enjoy their boat all summer. Their three kids, Jennifer (age 10), Johnny (age 8), and Francine (age 5) are good students at school where they are active in sports and clubs. Here is their story.

Friday night

7:15 p.m.   Mary Hackell heads to the store to purchase snacks and goodies for the trip. She brims with excitement. Her shopping list is a mile long, but she is confident that it will go quickly.

7:42 p.m.   Bill checks his vast array of fishing equipment to be sure that everything is in good working order. He is also quite excited. He is not satisfied with the condition of the line in two of the reels so he restrings them. He has not stopped whistling since he left work at 5:15.

8:24 p.m. Mary returns from shopping and begins to make sandwiches for the day ahead. It usually bothers her that none of her children like the same thing, but this time she doesn't seem to mind making fourteen sandwiches- each of them different.

8:45 p.m. Bill finishes working on the fishing equipment. The reels are restrung and the lures are meticulously placed in the tackle box in size order. He has still not stopped whistling. He loads it all into the minivan.

8:51p.m Bill packs a cooler of soda, beer and perishable foodstuffs while Mary finishes making the sandwiches. Everything they will need for the excursion is neatly placed by the front door.

9:48p.m. Everyone falls into bed anxiously awaiting morning.

Saturday Morning

6:00a.m. The alarm clock screeches with a shrill that could wake the dead.

6:03a.m. Bill stumbles toward the bathroom in a groggy haze. His hair stands straight up and he's rubbing his eyes with the ferocity of a lion on a kill.

6:03a.m. Bill trips over one of Jennifer's skates and lands heavily on the floor but not before completely leveling out horizontally while in mid air.

6:04a.m. Bill uses the F- word for the first time of the day.

6:18a.m. Everybody is more or less awake and getting dressed. Bill's mood has improved somewhat but he is walking with a slight limp.

6:53a.m. The car is packed and the whole family gets in. There are smiling faces throughout the car. Even Bill is smiling despite a sharp pain that shoots up his spine.

7:12a.m. The Hackells arrive at the Marina. The kids jump out of the minivan squealing in glee. The parents have to shout to remind them not to go to the boat empty-handed.

7:22a.m. Everything is on the boat. The kids have their life vests on and sit on the bow giggling and laughing amongst themselves. Bill and Mary stop for a brief moment to smile at each other. They appear to be the perfect family having a perfect day.

7:23a.m. The engine won't start.

7:45a.m. Bill waits for the Marina's ships store to open. After fifteen minutes slung over the engine, he discovers that an obscure part on the bottom of the motor has expired. Fortunately the part is relatively inexpensive and he is almost sure that the marina will keep it in stock.

8:10a.m. The store is open and Bill has found his part. It cost only $3.25. However, he discovers that in order to install the part, he must also buy a tool that costs $130.00. This tool will never again be of any use to him.

8:42a.m .The part has been replaced and the family is now departing the marina and heading for the open water which lies just ahead.

8:57a.m. Bill misjudges the size of a wake that was left by another boat which is now a quarter of a mile away. Instead of taking the wake at an angle, he hits it dead on. Francine, who is sitting on the bow, bounces a full two feet out of her seat and lands rather hard on her backside. She cries hysterically. Her screams almost achieve almost the same volume as the icy looks that Bill is receiving from Mary.

9:02a.m. Francine has not stopped crying. Mary is no longer satisfied with simply giving Bill icy stares so she begins a tirade about Bill's boat handling, bringing up incidents from two seasons earlier.

9:05a.m. Bill now becomes defensive and the first fight of the day begins.

9:14a.m. The fight ends in a stalemate. The trip resumes.

9:44a.m.   They arrive at their first destination, a beach where many local boaters go to drop anchor and swim. Bill drops the anchor and checks it to make sure that it grabbed the bottom. It did. The kids have been complaining about hunger for fifteen minutes so Mary serves them cereal that she packed the night before.

9:48a.m.   They get hit with a wake from another arriving boat. Two cereal bowls fly into the air while the third drops straight to the floor. Now it's Bill's turn to shoot a look to Mary. He gives her the rare, yet distinct "why the hell did you bring cereal out on a boat" look.

10:02a.m.   The mess has been cleaned up and the children are now eating candy.

10:13a.m.   Breakfast is over and Johnny jumps in for a swim.

10:19a.m.   Johnny cramps up while swimming (it appears that there is some degree of truth to the "half-hour rule"). Bill smashes his knee on the gunnel as he dives overboard to rescue him.

10:22a.m.   Johnny is back aboard and panting heavily, he bears a strong resemblance to a drowning rat. Bill feels the first shot of pain in his knee since it splintered the wood trim on the starboard side of his boat. The only thing that makes him momentarily forget his pain is the realization that his watch is no longer on his wrist. Bill uses the f-word for the second time of the day.

10:36a.m. Johnny is dry and breathing much more normally. He has vomited twice, but Mary cleaned it up right away. Everything seems to be back to normal, except that Bill's limp has become somewhat more pronounced.

10:57a.m. The decision is made to do some knee boarding. The family has moved to a quiet bay about two miles from the beach. Jennifer demands that she go first. She jumps in the water with the kneeboard and the boat moves into position with Mary at the helm and Bill serving as the lookout.

11:16a.m. Jennifer has been knee boarding for almost three miles. She is an excellent knee boarder and has even done a few tricks.

11:20a.m. Johnny and Francine whine for potato chips. While Mary concentrates on the water ahead, Bill momentarily takes his eyes from Jennifer to dig the potato chips out from the bottom of the supply cabinet. Although it was only for a minute or so, it was enough time for Jennifer to fall off the kneeboard, become entangled in the towline, and be dragged for a half mile.

11:21a.m. Mary gives a casual look over her shoulder only to see the tops of Jennifer's feet being dragged behind the boat.

11:24a.m.   Jennifer is recovered and pulled aboard. She is coughing and vomiting, but Bill notes that she'll be all right. Mary launches a verbal onslaught at Bill that causes him to step back reflexively.

11:25a.m.   A loud and animated argument ensues. It involves not only the matter at hand, but reaches topics as unrelated as Bill's excessive flatulation in bed and Mary's annoying brother.

12:09p.m.   The argument is over and Mary has won. Bill limps over to the cooler and grabs a beer, muttering under his breath.

12:20p.m.   It is lunchtime. The family goes back to the beach and ravenously devour the sandwiches that Mary prepared the night before.

1:18p.m.   Lunch is over. It was uneventful save for the fact that Bill and Mary did not speak a word to each other the entire time. They did deliver messages to each other by passing comments to the kids so that the other could hear them.

1:52p.m.   The kids are swimming around the boat. From the port side can be heard, "Marco" and the response, "Polo" can be heard from starboard. Everything would appear normal, but Bill and Mary are at opposite ends of the boat and still haven't said a word to each other. Bill is on his third beer, and Mary is almost finished with her first glass of wine.

2:09p.m.   The kids want to see a natural rock formation that lies on the shoreline about eighteen miles away. It forms a slide that lands in the water and every kid in the area talks about it. It is one of the spots that Bill had originally intended to visit, but the pain in his leg has gotten worse so he was hoping to forego the journey. He looks over at his wife and thinks that his pain in the ass is still here, too. He smiles to himself. He agrees to go and Mary just shrugs.

2:34p.m.   They are running at three quarters throttle towards the rock formation and the boat is doing about thirty knots. Bill is at the helm and notices Mary precariously leaning over to retrieve some pretzels for the kids. He also spots a series of six-inch waves ahead that are caused by the wind. He immediately cuts back the throttle and the boat comes to an abrupt halt. Mary goes "ass over teakettle" into the windscreen. She lies on the deck among the potato chips that were in the 2 lb. unopened bags that broke her fall. The bags exploded like M-80's when she hit them. Bill expresses concern, knowing that this worked better than intended and his intent could never be proven.

2:39p.m.   Another fight ensues. Bill only half defends himself, smiling smugly as he drinks his beer. Now Mary is also walking with a limp.

3:01p.m.   The Hackells have arrived at the rock formation and the kids are all over it.

3:38p.m. Johnny falls off a high point of the formation onto the rocks below. His pupils are dilated and his speech is slurred so they all decide that it would be wise to leave and go fishing.

4:19p.m. They arrive at one of Bill's favorite fishing holes. There are several boats there and they appear to be doing quite well. Bill quickly breaks out the fishing gear and distributes it to the family. Everyone begins fishing except Johnny, who is catatonic on the bow.

4:50p.m. Several fish have been brought aboard to the delight of the family. Johnny appears to be unconscious on the bow, but nobody notices. They are a family again.

5:19p.m. Bill cannot walk straight. It is unknown if this is a result of the pain he is feeling in his leg or the numbness that has been induced by the beer. Mary prepares to cast her line, but stumbles over the empty bottle of wine at her feet. The lure swings wildly behind her like an angry hornet and catches Jennifer on the scalp. Mary yanks the line and takes a two-inch piece of Jennifer's scalp with it.

5:22p.m. All poles are on the deck and the family runs around in a panic attempting to administer first aid to Jennifer. As is the case with many head wounds, there is profuse bleeding. Bill slips on the blood and smashes his shoulder against the steering column, knocking out the alignment in both the steering column and his shoulder. He has also hit the side of his head against the windshield. He can no longer hear the mayhem that is taking place all around him as his ears are filled with blood. Johnny has not regained consciousness, and has begun breathing very erratically.

5:44p.m. The bleeding from Jennifer's head has been contained. She is covered with blood and is still crying. She reminds Mary of the character in the movie Carrie. Johnny is now awake but his eyes keeping rolling spastically back into his head and he addresses everybody as "Aunt Petunia." Aunt Petunia died several years ago.

5:51p.m. It is unanimously decided by everyone who can speak that they should now go home. Bill staggers or limps over to the console and starts the engine, turning the key with his one good arm. He discovers that the steering has been damaged worse than he thought and the wheel can only turn about two degrees. He uses the F-word many, many times and calls for a tow.

7:35p.m. The towing company has finally arrived and has begun setting up a bridle. Nobody notices little Francine curled up in the head shivering like a chihua hua. She has received second-degree burns from the sun.

9:46p.m. They arrive back at the marina and tie off in their slip. Bill looks for his wallet to pay the tow-guy and realizes that his wallet is in the pocket of the pants he was wearing when he dove in the water after Johnny this morning. His wallet is soaked and his credit cards have fallen apart. Nobody finds this even remotely amusing, especially the tow guy. He and Bill argue for several minutes until they agree that the tow guy will come home with them to get the numbers from Mary's credit card that is in her wallet on the dining room table. Billy is now speaking in tongues.

9:59p.m.   The whole family and the tow guy hop into the minivan and head to the Hackell's house.

10:18p.m.   They arrive at the house and Bill runs in to get Mary's credit card, which he uses to pay the tow guy. The piece of Jennifer's scalp has fallen off again and Johnny is drooling uncontrollably. Mary decides to take them to the hospital in the other car while Bill brings the tow guy back to the marina and close up the boat.

1:30a.m.   The family is at home minus Johnny, who is staying overnight at the hospital for a few tests. Jennifer has an appointment on Tuesday for plastic surgery and Francine is covered from head to foot with some oily cream that the doctor has given her for sunburn. Bill curls up for a much needed night's sleep on the couch.

Epilogue

Wednesday

1:30p.m.   Jennifer's surgery went splendidly– very little permanent scarring will occur. Francine can still only wear loose-fitting sundresses but has begun peeling so the end of her misery is in sight. Johnny can now do simple arithmetic and the doctor has explained that the central nervous system is way over-rated anyway. Bill's arm is in a sling and he still has a slight limp, but he feels much better and thinks that this might actually improve his golf swing. Mary doesn't remember a thing that happened after her fourth glass of wine.

Thursday

5:39p.m.   Marina staff notice that there is smoke coming out of the Hackells boat. Despite valiant efforts made by them, the boat becomes fully engulfed in flames and ultimately sinks. It was later determined that arson was the cause. Bill Hackell comes under immediate suspicion as an eyewitness reported seeing a minivan similar to the Hackell's racing away moments before the smoke was noticed.

Boating Quiz #3

It's the end of the season and you pull your boat out of the water. You notice that the hull is completely covered in barnacles. Do you

a) Immediately dive underneath and begin scraping it

b) Leave it for next year

c) Go inside the boat club and discuss it over a few beers

Correct Answer is C- No boater wants the last memory of the season to be barnacle scraping, but you can't wait until next year having it bother you all winter. The only way to come up with a solution is to ask the other boating experts at the bar.

Years ago, pleasure boating was considered to be a pastime reserved for the young. Even today, it involves a lot of physical effort. However, it also involves a lot of money and this is an area where the old beat the young hands down. In fact, if the old have enough money, they can pay the young to do all the work for them so they can relax and enjoy their boats. That's real pleasure boating. Once the old realized this, they began buying boats in droves.

This change in the average age of boaters can be traced back to Jacques Cousteau. Cousteau was tooling around in his boat decades after he looked remotely good in a bathing suit. Despite all his travels, you never once saw him repairing an engine. It was always the young guys on the payroll who went below deck and sucked exhaust fumes every time there was a breakdown. Jacques would never dream of scraping barnacles. In fact, if he hadn't done a special on them, I doubt he would have even known what a barnacle was. You see, he had the right idea- pay someone else to do it. This enabled him to continue boating until he was well into his eighties. If he had had to change his own oil all those years he certainly would have stroked-out long before his time.

Inventions for Elderly Boaters

1.   Wheelchair ramp on the transom

2.   Glass jars permanently affixed to berths for teeth

3.   Vap-o-rub on the benches

4.   Captain's chair is a rocker

5.   Medic alerts on the PFDs

6.   Automatic stairway chair to the fly bridge

7.   Orthopedic boat shoes

8.   Hand rails on the porto-potty

9.   Prescription wind screen

10.   Ben Gay dispensers in the head

11.   Large print on the users manual

12.   Magnified glass on the gauges

How To Tell That Your Boat Club has an Older Membership

1.　　　Early bird specials in the kitchen

2.　　　Nap hour between 2 and 3pm

3.　　　Tuesday is bingo night

4.　　　Soda machine has a slot for prune juice

5.　　　Boat trips to the casino

6.　　　Ship's store sells blue wigs

7.　　　Sock garters are approved boating wear

8.　　　Juke box has nothing but Glen Miller Songs

9.　　　Eight people are needed to hoist the flag

10.　　Member discounts at the funeral home

"That's it!!!
No more upgrades!!!"

Topics of Conversation Held by the Old Timers at the Dock

1. The wonders of viagra

2. The new, designer "wonder truss" by Armani

3. Saltwater chafing

4. How sometimes their little engines just can't

5. Male pattern baldness

6. Controlled nuclear fission and its impact on the fragile waterway ecosystem

7. Secret attractions to Barbara Bush

8. Fourteen recipes involving prunes

9. Breakthroughs in carbuncle lancing

10. That despite advancing age, they're still just a bunch of crazy kids

Top Tens of Boating

(more or less)

Top Ten Sure Ways to Annoy the Skipper

1. Pull down his shorts while he maneuvers through rough water

2. Pour water on his seat whenever he stands up

3. Say, "Roger, Roger" every time he uses the VHF radio

4. Stand up and block his view whenever he looks over his shoulder to see behind the boat

5. Look overboard and yell, "Oh my God!!!"

6. Leave the water running in the sinks every time you use them

7. Tuck a newspaper under your arm and walk into the head

8. Play Jingle Bells on the air horn

9. Tell him that if you had a boat, it would be much bigger than his

10. No matter how fast he's going, tell him to slow down

Eleven Things That Never Made it in the Boating Industry

1. Edible bumpers

2. Salvation Navy

3. Free Tow

4. Johnson heat exchanger and popcorn maker

5. Amphibidingy

6. Hummingbird fish and Hoffa finder

7. U.S. Powder Squadron

8. The Hula Gasket

9. Bottom-friendly floating anchors

10. Personal Flotation Bricks (PFB's)

11. Fisher-Price junior flair gun

Ten Boating Phrases That Sound Dirty, But Really Aren't

1. "You really should see his Johnson"

2. "She'll always bring you home"

3. "I'm having a party down below"

4. "She just let fly"

5. "Pull this"

6. "She gives a pretty bumpy ride"

7. "Reach underneath and see what you feel"

8. "She rides great when she lays down flat"

9. "I think there's a problem with my lower unit"

10. "She's holding a lot of water lately"

Thirteen Ancient Myths of the Sea

1. Sea Serpents

2. Mermaids

3. Sea Sirens

4. 24 hour gas docks

5. The guy who fixed everything on his boat and now it runs perfectly

6. The dry bilge

7. The cheap marine store

8. Guests who buy gas

9. The free tow home

10. Dry boat clubs

11. No wake zones

12. The marine mechanic who doesn't show the crack of his ass every time he bends over

13. The Cigarette Boat owner who's not middle aged and divorced

Twenty-Five Concept Boats That Were Rejected by the Major Manufacturers

1. The Tupper-Tug
2. The Cardboard Cutter
3. The Pumice Pro
4. The Envirokiller
5. Lead Lucy
6. Sea Slug
7. The Casket Cruiser
8. Sun Hog
9. Hydro-Hippo
10. PCB Churner
11. Paper Pro
12. Pudding Runner
13. Leak Master
14. Road Rage
15. Burn Deck
16. Break Drive
17. The Gut Gunnels
18. Slush Deck
19. Bilge Runner
20. Gas Raider
21. Money Bridge
22. Oil Skeg
23. Cash Classic
24. Rogue Reflux
25. Arthroscopic Express

Famous Last Words

1. "So what, it's only an iceberg"

2. "That's not a periscope, it's probably only a log."

3. "What'dya mean the cook always goes down with the ship?"

4. "What's this plug for?"

5. "How much could they possibly charge for a tow?"

6. "Don't worry, we have plenty of gas."

7. "The weatherman always exaggerates about these storms..."

8. "The guy at the boat show said it hardly uses any gas at all."

9. "Don't worry, honey. I'll just buy it and if you don't like it, I'll sell it."

Fourteen Acronyms for the Word B.O.A.T.

1.   Break Out Another Thousand

2.   Beginnings Of A Tic

3.   Bring Out A Telephone

4.   Broken On A Tide

5.   Bank On A Tow

6.   Bend Over Another Time

7.   Big Oily After-Thought

8.   Beware Of Airborne Toupees

9.   Bills Over-Accrue Terribly

10.   Bring Oars And Tents

11.   Bringing On A Tantrum

12.   Big, Oblong Adult Toy

13.   Blacked Out At Boatshow

14.   Bring On Another Tax

Top Ten Power Squadron Courses We Could Really Use

1. Starboard & Port: Let's Get It Right Once and For All

2. Boating: It's Even Fun When You're Sober

3. How To Tell Your Kids That They Can't Use Your Boat

4. How To Get Cheap %&^#@! Guests To Pay For Gas

5. Shallow Water: Looks Just Like Deep Water Only Shallower

6. You & Your Boat: A Study In Needless Spending

7. Gas siphoning 101

8. Reaching The Last Bolt On The Starter Motor Through Yoga

9. Your Kids College Fund: A Potential Down Payment On The New Boat

10. Peculiar Smells That Can Kill You

Similarities Between Marina Owners and Undertakers

1. They both drain your blood

2. They both can bury you pretty much when they want

3. They park you for a while and then get rid of you

4. You almost never hear them laugh

5. They have one office that you can enter and another one that you can never see

6. They seem apologetic when handing you the bill

7. They both laugh at you when you're naked

8. They rarely go to the circus

9. They seem to wear the same clothes day after day

10. They always carry handkerchiefs

Top Ten Acronyms for P.C.B.

1. Petroleum Colored Black

2. Produces Carbuncles and Blisters

3. Paisley Crabs on Bottom

4. People Can Barf

5. Poor Catfish are Blind

6. Probably Can't Biodegrade

7. Puts Chromosomes at Bay

8. Pretty Cruddy Bottom

9. Prevents Conception of Babies

10. Pregnancy Can't Begin

Best of Cap'n Drew's

Classic
Reader Letters

Dear Cap'n Drew: I have been considering buying a boat for several years, but have never had enough courage to actually go through with it. Is there any advice you could give to encourage me? - Frank in Haverstraw

Dear Frank: The problem seems to be simply that you are just very cheap. You must break out the crowbar and pry that wallet open. Take a leap of faith.

Dear Cap'n Drew: What is the difference between miles-per-hour and knots? - Bill in Tarrytown

Dear Bill: Miles-per-hour is how many miles someone or something goes in one hours time. A knot is something you tie with a rope. Duh.

Dear Cap'n Drew: I was told by a marine repairman that there was a problem with my intermediate housing. I'm embarrassed to say that I don't even know where this is. Can you please tell me? - D.M. from Fishkill

Dear D.M.: Intermediate housing is located somewhere between the government assisted housing and Beverly Hills.
I don't think I understand your question.

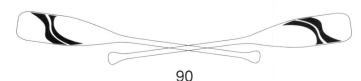

Dear Cap'n Drew: My wife and I are inviting all of our friends out on our twenty-two footer for an autumn cruise. What type of food should we serve?
-Confused in Dutchess

Dear Confused: If all of your friends fit on a twenty-two footer, your problem isn't simply a matter of social etiquette. Try joining a social group and buying a few rounds.

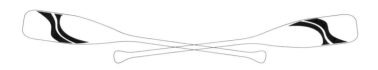

Dear Cap'n Drew: I have been reading about plans to build more nuclear power plants along the Hudson River over the next few years. What is your opinion of this? - Eddie in Haverstraw

Dear Eddie: Although we are told that nuclear power is the safest form of energy, I have yet to see anybody wearing those big white suits for a coal leak. I occasionally ponder as to what effect controlled nuclear explosions in the neighborhood will have on the fifth generation family gerbil. It seems, however, that the biggest problem that the State Legislature is having on this issue is what to name the booming "Nuke Towns" that rise up around such power plants. On the condition of anonymity, my sources in Albany have given me some of the names that are being considered:

Top Ten Names for "Nuke Towns" on the Waterways

1. Plutonium Plains

2. Microwave Meadows

3. Strontium Springs

4. Reactorsburgh

5. Half-Life Hills

6. Deformity Cove

7. Fallout Falls

8. Cooling Tower Crossing

9. Meltdown Mews

10. Third Eye Junction

Dear Cap'n Drew: I was recently told that all children are required to wear flotation while on a boat. Is this true?
-Kim from Newburgh

Dear Kim: While it is true that children are required to wear flotation when on a boat, it is a little known fact that children actually serve as excellent flotation for adults during an emergency (especially the chubby kids). I have heard numerous stories of people surviving for days at sea with nothing more than a bottle of water and a plump, buoyant toddler.

Dear Cap'n Drew: Why are elevated helms called "Fly Bridges?" -Jeff from Yonkers

Dear Jeff: Elevated helms got their nickname "Fly Bridges" after the much hated green flies who often patrol at altitude and bite unwary skippers on the ass. They were dubbed this after an incident in 1963 where a pleasure boat Captain cruised his boat into green fly territory in the inland waterway somewhere down south. He was swarmed by thousands of the vile creatures and skeletonized in a matter of minutes-while his poor, unsuspecting wife sat below deck making a fondue.

Dear Cap'n Drew: Why do Navy uniforms look so unusual. No other branch of the military requires that its people wear bell-bottoms or those round hats. I was told that the reason they look the way that they do was for functionality, although I can't imagine what that could be.
- Patti in Scotia, NY

Dear Patti: It is absolutely true that Navy uniforms were designed for functionality. The Navy Department came up with the design many years ago after a severe outbreak of social disease caused several ships to be held up in port. After this, the Navy began dressing its sailors up to look so silly that no woman in any port would look at them seriously.

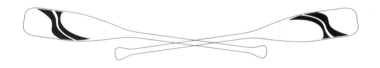

Dear Cap'n Drew: Every spring, when I put my boat in the water, a duck promptly lays her eggs in it. When I attempt to board my boat, she becomes very agitated and attempts to bite me. Is there anything I can do to prevent this next year? - Dave in Albany

Dear Dave: It is a widely known fact that, in Duckdom, females (also known as "duckettes") will lay eggs only in the territory of males (also known as "bull ducks") for whom they have no respect. I think that, in order to remedy this problem in the future, you might want to take a course in self-confidence since you obviously don't get any respect from even the lowest members of the food chain.

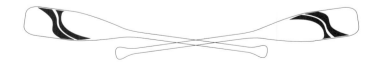

"Heathens"

Dear Cap'n Drew: My wife and I occasionally sleep on our boat while it is tied to the slip at our marina. It seems that almost every time we do this, our neighbor in the slip next to us is having a party in his boat with several people and loud music, keeping us awake all night. We have tried dropping hints to him, but he doesn't seem to pick them up. We've even mentioned it to the owner of the marina who tells us that he'll say something to them the next time he hears such a party going on. This has yet to happen. It has come to the point where my wife and I won't sleep on our boat any more. This really bothers me since we really enjoy sleeping out and don't feel that we should suffer because we're stuck next to this guy. What should we do?

-Sleepless on the Hudson

Dear Sleepless: It seems as though you have tried every socially acceptable means possible to shut this lout up. Remember, when the methods of polite society fail, the rules of the schoolyard will prevail. Go to your local pet store and pick up about a half dozen crickets (pet stores keep plenty of them on hand to sell as food for various pets). Bring them to the marina and, when you're sure that this guy is not around, release them in his boat. If you've ever had even one of the little buggers loose in your living room, you know that they have the noise making power of a twelve piece band. They will find every nook and cranny of the boat, live on the many crumbs found there and chirp all night. That will be the last good sleep HE gets on a boat for a while. Don't worry about the crickets, either. Once the food supply runs out, they'll find their way off the boat and move on to greener pastures. By the way, when you renew your membership at the marina next year, demand a slip as far from the guy as possible.

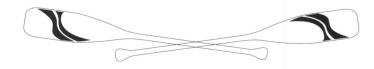

Dear Cap'n Drew: Last year I broke down on the water and was towed home by a passing boater. I was very glad for the help until he charged me $200 for the tow! I thought that boaters were supposed to tow each other out of courtesy. What are your thoughts? -Chris in Massapequa

Dear Chris: As my grandmother used to say, "There's one in every crowd." Just be glad that you got home. Look at the bright side, when you call them, you can give your kids a great lesson on capitalism.

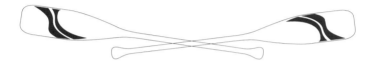

Jobs in Hell For Boaters Who Charge Other Boaters For A Tow

1. Seeing eye dog repossessor

2. Collector for bookies

3. Bouncer at the nursing home

4. Prostate checker

5. Chief executioner at the dog pound

6. Orphanage forecloser

7. Animal tester at a cosmetics lab

8. Lollipop repossessor

9. Seal clubber

10. Bunny rabbit euthanizer at the petting zoo

11. Disability claim denier for the Social Security Department

Dear Cap'n Drew: Why are British sailors referred to as "Limeys?" I've heard this expression many times, but cannot figure out what its origins could be... -Jay in Wurtsboro

Dear Jay: This is a very interesting question. British sailors have had this nickname for over two hundred years. They were dubbed "Limeys" because of the British Navy's practice of carrying limes aboard their ships. Due to a lack of proper nutrition, many sailors of the day would contract a disease called scurvy. Scurvy is caused by a lack of vitamin C in the diet and was widespread at the time. Since limes stay fresh for a considerable amount of time, the British Navy would carry them in the ships hold and feed them to the sailors to prevent the disease. Today, however, the Navy finds it more appropriate to carry penicillin to fight the diseases contracted by its sailors.

Dear Cap'n Drew: I was recently informed that fois gras with an insouciant little white wine is better on hot, sunny yachting days while caviar is more favorable in cloudy weather. What do you recommend? -Charles H. in Manhattan

Dear Charles: W-h-a-a-a-a-a-t?

Dear Cap'n Drew: Last summer I tried a stainless steel prop. My boat is a 2000 Sea Ray that came with a 23-degree aluminum prop. I tried the same pitch prop in stainless steel and to my surprise, my top end decreased 1 or 2 mph and my RPM's decreased by 500 RPM. I'm confused as to why this happened. I thought that my top speed would have gone up. Do you have any insight why this happened? -Bill S. in Castleton, NY

Dear Bill: It seems as though you might have fallen victim to a band of black market bootleggers who pass off bogus stainless steel props to unsuspecting boaters.   These fake props are typically made of plastic that is painted a shiny silver color. To determine whether you have one of these counterfeits, look at the inside hub- if you see the words "Fisher Price," you probably have a fake. Don't feel that you are alone.   These scoundrels have been victimizing people all over the Hudson and the entire East Coast. They have even been know to sell these fake props to little old ladies on fixed incomes and very little savings – who probably only needed aluminum props to begin with. Public Service Announcement – If you think that you have been victimized by the fake prop gang- call the New York State Steel Prop Fraud Unit at (800) 555-screw.

Dear Cap'n Drew: I have been reading your column for some time now and would like to share a story with you.

In the fall, I was out on my 24-footer with my wife, her brother and sister and their spouses. We went out for an evening cruise to sip wine and watch the sun set. We turned off the engine at around 6:30 and watched natures wonder. However, when we prepared to go back in, the engine wouldn't turn over. We sat for a few minutes attempting to reach the Coast Guard on the VHF when, suddenly we discovered a leak in the hull. The water grew deeper and deeper in the boat until the boat finally began to list to one side and ultimately sank. At this point we were finally forced to swim to shore and call the authorities. What do you think about THAT for a night out?
-Soaked in Poughkeepsie, NY

Dear Soaked: Aside from all that, what did you think of the play, Mrs. Lincoln?

Dear Cap'n Drew: With the start of a new season, my husband and I were hoping that you might have any tips on how to clean a porta-potty without getting filthy.
   -Grossed out in Kingston, NY

Dear Grossed: That's an easy one. Have your kids do it.

Dear Cap'n Drew: My husband is a die-hard fisherman. He has been fishing in the Hudson River for many years. He is always pressuring me to buy him very expensive equipment that will help him locate fish. Cap'n Drew, does this stuff really work or would I just be throwing good money down the drain?   -Fishing Widow in Weehawken, NJ

Dear Widow: The truth is- there really are no fish in the Hudson. I have been fishing in the Hudson for over a decade and have never caught a thing. Your husband is probably having an affair. I recommend that you find a good divorce lawyer and rake him over the coals. He should have come up with a more believable excuse.

Dear Cap'n Drew: My husband and I often debate over what can be considered proper boating attire. What do you consider good "boating wear?"
-Spiffy in Staten Island

Dear Spiffy: Until last year, I would sport a thong while cruising around on my boat. This lasted until I was harpooned in the buttocks by Norwegian Whale Poachers who were patrolling in the Hudson. It is a little known fact that a very similar incident happened to Hendrick Hudson, for whom the Hudson River is named, which is the reason his ship was named the Half Moon.

Dear Cap'n Drew: Recently I took my boat down below Manhattan to do some early season fishing. I didn't have charts for the area, but I stayed near other boats and kept a watchful eye on the markers. The day started fine, but within an hour, a boat went by at high speed rocking me with its wake. When I looked over, everyone on the boat yelled at me as though I had done something wrong. Several similar incidents like this occurred including one where a boat went by and everyone aboard stood up and "gave me the finger." I have never experienced such rude boaters in all my life. I've looked at charts and maps since then, but I still can't figure out exactly where I was. Do you have any ideas?

-Shocked in the Hudson

Dear Shocked: There is only one place that you could have been – Brooklyn, NY. Brooklyn is a strange land with truly unique inhabitants. Having grown up there, I am familiar with its customs and traditions. For example, when we played football in high school, after tackling the quarterback, we went after his family. Don't be offended by the behavior of the aborigines. In Brooklyn, "giving the finger" is like a friendly wave...

Eleven Indications That You Might Be Boating in Brooklyn:

1. All radio transmissions begin with, "Yo."

2. The clams are wearing tank tops.

3. When the weather station broadcasts a small craft warning advising all boats to find shelter, the response is, "why don't YOU leave."

4. Those whitefish just can't seem to fight the tide.

5. There is graffiti on the buoys.

6. The guys next to you are fishing with shotguns.

7. Even the Coast Guard says, "Fuhgeddaboutit."

8. When you catch and release a fish, he tells you that he's "comin' back with the boys."

9. You notice that even the seagulls have tattoos.

10. The party boats are using a guy named Vito as chum.

11. The twelve o'clock whistle is the theme to "The Godfather."

Dear Cap'n Drew: I have a windlass on my boat and my best friend (who, incidentally, docks right next to me) tells me that I'm lazy for using it. Personally, I think that it is the best thing that I have ever bought. However, I'm starting to think that my buddy is right and that I should haul the anchor myself. Cap'n Drew, is it wrong to use mechanical devices such as these or should I "rough it?"
Signed, Lazy in Chelsea, NY

Dear Lazy: Due to the complexity of your situation, I gathered my team of world-renowned psychologists on the matter. After an evening of sitting around and discussing your case while smoking Optimos (world-renowned psychologists are known for smoking very cheap cigars) it was decided that your friend has an extreme case of "windlass envy." It was also determined that there is very little that you can do about it. Perhaps, the next time he gives you grief about using a windlass, you should whip out a pay stub or a tax return and ask him to compare – he'll shut-up.

This reminds me of when I was first married. Many of my friends called their wives and girlfriends "pooky" or "Shmooky," I nicknamed my wife "windlass." I truly thought that this was very practical.

She hit me with a waffle iron.

Dear Cap'n Drew: While cruising around New York Harbor, I spotted a very unusual looking sailboat. A friend who was out with me called it a "Chinese Junk." Is this actually a type of sailboat, or was he just making it up?
-Puzzled in Manhattan

Dear Puzzled: In truth, there is no sailboat design of that name. Your friend is obviously a patriotic American. He knows that until the Government of China abandons Communism and adopts Capitalism, they will be destined to manufacture nothing but junk. Your friend was simply describing the quality of products that are produced by Communist nations. For example, when you walk through a dollar store, you see aisle upon aisle of "Chinese Junk." You get the picture.

Dear Cap'n Drew: When you spoke about legends of the sea in your last column, you forgot to mention the Giant Squid. How could you forget a big one like that?
-Calamari lover in Beacon

Dear Cal: I didn't include it in the column because there is now very little doubt in Oceanographic circles that they actually exist. The Giant Squid isn't really considered to be a myth anymore. Cap'n Drew has known this for some time, however, as I actually dated one for a while in college.

Dear Cap'n Drew: How do I align the shaft and the engine on a 28 foot cruiser? The engine is a Chrysler 318 V-8 inboard with a straight shaft. I removed both the shaft and the engine in order to do fiberglass work in my transom. Since I reinstalled it, the boat has had a wicked shimmy. I am afraid to push it up over 4 knots. How do I fix this? -Milo Connecticut

Dear Milo: Let's get one thing straight from the beginning- nobody uses the word "wicked" anymore. Even in the last Wizard of OZ remake, they described the witch as "bitchy." Secondly, why are you pulling things apart that you don't know how to reassemble? Didn't you ever get whacked for doing that to a household appliance when you were a kid?

It's against my better judgment, but I'll help you anyway. Read the following carefully:

First- take the straight shaft and graft it to the flux capacitor. Then run a link from that junction to the warp drive (this will prevent the cavitations). You will now see a slight gap in the transmission flange. This is OK- simply install a left-handed sky hook (of medium size) into the gap. This will eliminate the shimmy and insure the smooth running of your boat. A word of caution: If you are able to complete this-please do your shake down cruise without your children.

Dear Cap'n Drew: I was out for a boat ride with my family the other night near Newburgh. When I was pulling my boat out of the water, I overheard a man on the dock say that he recently saw a four-foot sturgeon while fishing on the Hudson. Are there still sturgeon of this size in the Hudson? I thought that they had been gone for years.
-Fishfinder in Dutchess

Dear Fish: What you probably heard was that the man saw a four-foot surgeon who was fishing in the Hudson. The northeast United States has a higher percentage of dwarfs who are in the medical profession than any other area of the country. So next time you see a "little person" out fishing, be sure to give a friendly smile and a wave. If you ever get wheeled into the hospital with a ruptured appendix, he could be the guy hovering over you with a scalpel (on a step stool).

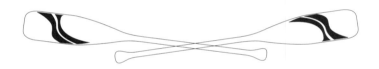

Dear Cap'n Drew: I have a friend who has a boat that is the same size as mine, but he always calls his boat a yacht. I think that he has delusions of grandeur, but he insists that he has "yacht status." At what point can a boat be called a yacht?
-Ray in the Bronx

Dear Ray: If you have to ask, it's a boat.

Dear Cap'n Drew: My husband has been talking about buying an autopilot system for our boat for quite a while. I'm not so sure it's a good idea. What do you think?
-Kim in New Jersey

Dear Kim: I'm with you. Most people wouldn't allow their best friend to borrow their boat, yet they permit a computer with the decision-making ability of an automatic door to pilot it. If you don't enjoy being at the helm of your own boat, then throw an anchor.

Dear Cap'n Drew: I was given a 1972 Grand Banks Trawler by my uncle who could no longer afford the storage. It has not been the water for over ten years and needs a considerable amount of work on the hull cabin and engines. I plan to begin refurbishing it this winter and wanted to see if you might suggest any books that would assist me in such an endeavor.
-George in New Jersey

Dear George: You might want to consider the Bible. I think you're gonna need a lot of prayers to get you through this one. You also might want to use the phone book to look up a boat broker to call when you finally get disgusted and want to buy a new one.

Dear Cap'n Drew: I was at a boat show this year and actually saw a boat with a goldfish tank on board. Is this common on larger boats? It seems that it can't be good for the fish.
-Something's fishy in Jersey

Dear Fishy: I feel that keeping fish in a bowl is a terribly cruel thing to do, whether it's on a boat or in your home. They spend their entire lives in a tiny glass bubble banging into the glass walls. Goldfish are the "bubble boys" of the animal kingdom. Everybody feels sorry for human bubble boys, but nobody ever lift a finger to help captive fish. Nature never intended for goldfish to eat flakes. They have survived for millions of years on their instincts. These instincts lead them to hunt and savagely kill their prey since they almost never find flakes in their wild ocean habitat. I believe that we should all unite and petition Amnesty International to stop this horror. Free the Goldfish.

Dear Cap'n Drew: My wife and I are looking to take up a hobby together. After much debate, we have narrowed our decision to boating and camping. We've shopped for boats and campers and they appear to be in the same price range. I'm in favor of buying a boat, but my wife is leaning towards a camper. Can you offer us any good advice to help us make up our minds?
-John in Glenmont

Dear John: As you might have guessed, I would be in favor of boating. Boating is like camping- except everybody has teeth. There also tends to be a considerable amount of added flexibility associated with boating. Anybody who has attempted to go camping after work on a Tuesday and get back by Wednesday morning can attest to this. In addition, when you're out on your boat and become tired of your guests, you can simply bring them home. If you go camping with friends, you're stuck with them for the duration. Camping isn't all bad mind you. In fact, I used to do it quite a bit. I slowed down on it considerably, however as a result of my last camping trip back in '91. Seems the yokel at the site next to mine sat up all night with his banjo- strumming the tune from "Deliverance."

"She may not be much to look at,
but she never gives me a hard time
about my boat."

Dear Cap'n Drew: My husband and I recently got back from a trip to Mexico. While walking along the beach, we saw the boats with the parasail rides all over the place. I wanted desperately to take a ride, but my husband refused. In fact, he gave me such a hard time about the whole thing that I ultimately gave up the idea. Do you think he was being unreasonable?   -Kate in Stillwater

Dear Kate: I'm afraid that I have to agree with him. I'm a firm believer in staying on "terra firma" - the more firma, the less terra. Besides, I tend to be a little nervous doing anything along those lines in a foreign country. Most countries don't exactly have the same safety guidelines for sports of this nature as we do here. The last time I was in Cancun I actually considered parasailing at one place until I got close and saw the line that they were using was just a bunch of old shoelaces tied together.

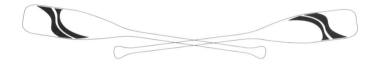

Dear Cap'n Drew: I wanted to share an idea with your readers. I ate at a diner in the beginning of the 1999 boating season and took home one of the placemat maps. The map was pretty detailed so I began using it as a chart when I went out on my boat. I used it all season and it worked just fine. In fact, I haven't had to buy a chart in two years! What do you think?
-Owen in Hopewell

Dear Owen: I think that you should probably be shot. Who did you eat with at the diner- the Captain of the Exxon Valdez?

Dear Cap'n Drew: There is always talk of requiring people to obtain licenses or certifications to operate boats. Do you think that this is a good idea?
-Bob in Monsey

Dear Bob: I think it's a great idea. Perhaps then we could lose Owen (see previous letter) from our midst. I certainly have no aversion to a written and on-water test. Boats are bigger and more dangerous than cars yet anybody with a few bucks can buy and use one. The state should obtain several test boats that are equipped with an ejector seat to catapult out anybody who makes three mistakes.

On-Board Cookin'

Cap'n Drew's Seafaring Recipes

Many boaters find on-board cooking to be among the most stressful aspects of boating. If you are among them, SNAP OUT OF IT!!! The simple truth is that guests don't expect to receive four-star meals when they come out on your boat. With the exception of cruise ships; boats are not designed with food preparation in mind. By and large, they are wobbly, rocking platforms with cooking facilities that one might find in the third world. Therefore, set your sights very low when considering the kind of food to serve guests who come boating. You must also learn how to manage your guests' expectations as to what will be served. If you are trying to impress your guests with your cooking, it is best done at home.

In the following pages you will find recipes with varying levels of complexity that are sure to tantalize your guests.

Complexity Rating Scale

1-   **Easiest**- can be prepared by most gorillas

2-   **Novice**- preparer must be a human being, but can be missing a chromosome or two

3-   **Intermediate**- cook must have basic understanding of the differences between salt and pepper.

4-   **Advanced**- must have logged at least ten lifetime hours watching Emeril

5-   **Expert**- someone who actually cooks once in a while

Potato Chips

Complexity rating- 1

Needed (serves 4):

1 twelve-ounce bag of potato chips

-Purchase potato chips
-Open Bag
-Pass bag around to guests*

Although this may seem extraordinarily easy, there are many people who cannot get even this right. Today's potato chips have gotten quite exotic in their flavorings and picking the wrong one might leave you with several guests who will not eat. Be careful not to select one that is too radical.

For example: While "Barbeque" flavored chips have become widely accepted, it would be wise not to choose the "Donkey's-Ass With A Touch of Lemon" flavored variety.

* *In the event that your guests are from more polite society, placing the chips in a bowl might be a welcome touch.*

Cheese & Crackers

Complexity rating- 2 (involves the using of a knife)

Needed (serves 4):

1 eight-ounce block of mild cheddar cheese
1 sixteen ounce box of crackers (Ritz or Townhouse)

-Slice cheese into slim, neat pieces

-Set on tray with crackers placing crackers in circular formation around the outside with cheese slices in the middle

-Serve to guests

Remember not to attempt to slice the cheese while the boat is underway. However, if you do, you will want to advise the guests that you will now be serving Cheese & Crackers & Thumbskin. If you say it quickly, it is unlikely that they will even notice what you have said.

Fried Chicken

Complexity rating- 1

Needed (serves 6-8):

1 large size bucket of chicken from KFC.
1 big thing of cole slaw
1 bunch of those biscuits

- Transfer items from boxes into personal tupperware the night before you go out
- Open on board claiming to have been cooking all night
- Serve on individual plates to guests

*Because of the extreme popularity of the Colonel's chicken, there is a chance that at least one of your guests will realize that what you are serving is actually the secret recipe. Be sure to smile and vehemently deny this. If that guest insists on pursuing the argument, "accidentally" bump into him so that he falls overboard. Whether the bump is seen as an accident or otherwise, the "chicken debate" will surely be dropped from that point forward.

Hamburgers

Complexity rating- 2 (requires careful timing)

Needed (serves 4):

4 ready made, cellophane wrapped, microwave burgers that can be found at the local Quickie Mart or 7-Eleven

-Wait for guests to go swimming
-Open bags and toss burgers into the microwave*
-When guests come out of the water, have burgers waiting for them on individual plates

Having returned from their swim to find these burgers waiting for them might raise a few inquiries from your guests. Simply tell them that you prepared them with your "On-Board Grilling System." If one of them asks to see this system, begin coughing convulsively as if you are choking. This should make her forget about the issue.

It should be noted that burgers of this type have a reputation for causing extreme gastritis. However this will not occur for several hours by which time your guests will have gone home and will just have to deal with each other.

If your boat is not equipped with a microwave, you can adequately warm the burgers by leaving them in their wrapping and placing one under each arm and sitting on the other two for approximately six minutes.

Shrimp In Wine

Complexity rating- 2

Needed (serves 4):

1 big package of pre-cleaned and cooked shrimp with cocktail
   sauce from the supermarket
3 bottles of wine

-First serve the wine in vast quantities
-When the guests appear to be "liquored up" serve the shrimp

**This system works extremely well since by the following morn-
ing, all that the guests can remember is that they were on a
boat and that they ate some shrimp- both of which are good
things. To avoid embarrassment, they will rave about what a
wonderful time they had with you as well as how good a cook
you are.**

Cap'n Drew's Barnacle Bisque

Complexity rating- 4

Needed (makes 4 bowls):
1 (10 Oz) can of condensed tomato soup
1 cup of fish broth
1 (10 oz) can of cream of mushroom
3 tablespoons of butter
1-1/2 cups of whole milk
1 onion (chopped large)
1-1/2 cups of crabmeat
1/4 cup of sliced almonds
1 cup of old barnacles scraped off of your boat

-Mix the butter, tomato soup, cream of mushroom soup, onion and the fish broth in a large pot and begin to cook over low heat for five minutes. Stir frequently.

-Add the whole milk and crabmeat- continue to cook for 5 minutes. Keep stirring.

-Add the sliced almonds, cook for 3 more minutes.

-Serve hot- stir before serving to get almonds in every bowl.

Place the soup bowls on small plates. Put a few tablespoons of the old barnacle scrapings on the plate with the bowl (you didn't think you were really going to eat them, did you?)

Each time your friends bite into an almond, be sure to tell them that it is one of the barnacles that you scraped off of the hull of your boat. They'll love it.

Cap'n Drew's Severed Mermaid Hands

Complexity rating- 3

Needed (serves 4):
4 tuna steaks
20 jumbo shrimp
2 tablespoons of lemon juice
10 oz. container of red cocktail sauce
1 tablespoon of onion powder
1 eight oz. bottle of teriyaki BBQ sauce
1 tablespoon of garlic powder
4 old rings (well cleaned)
4 parsley sprigs
2 tablespoons of chopped parsley

- Mix the lemon juice, onion powder, garlic powder, and teriyaki BBQ sauce together in a container.

- Marinate the tuna steak in the mix for at least 4 hours (the longer the better).

- Grill the tuna steaks to taste. * Note: the less time it spends on the grill, the tastier it will be. Pour marinate over steaks when you flip them.

- Simultaneously boil the shrimp. Be sure to watch them closely as they cook very quickly.

Place a tuna steak on the center of each plate. Then take five shrimp for each plate and arrange them around the tuna steak in the form of a hand. Pour the cocktail sauce on the plate at the "wrist" of each "hand" to mimic blood. Place a ring in one "finger" of each "hand." Place a sprig of parsley on each plate and sprinkle a pinch of chopped parsley around the plate.

Be sure to tell your friends that you paid poachers top dollar for the severed hands of these mermaids and that they have been outlawed because of the outcry from Greenpeace. You might also mention that they are considered to be a delicacy in Japan where it is believed that they make your penis grow larger.

Fish Giblets

Complexity rating- 5

Needed (serves 4):

4 whole fish (cleaned)
2 dozen mussels
1 tablespoons of butter
1 dozen clams (little neck)
1 onion (chopped large)
1-1/2 quarts of tomato sauce
1 clove of garlic (chopped small)

Teaspoon of salt
1 cup of crabmeat
Pinch of oregano

-Fillet the fish and cut fillets into half dollar sized pieces. Cut off the heads and tails and save.

-Wash mussels and clams.

-Mix all of the ingredients except the fish fillets into a large pot and cook over medium heat for 12 minutes stirring frequently. Be sure all of the clams and mussels have opened.

-Add the fish filets and cook for another 7 minutes stirring gently.

-Reduce heat and simmer for 3-4 more minutes.

-Remove the mussels and clams from their shells and place the meat back in the pot.

Place a fish head and tail on either end of each plate. Gently stir the pot ladle onto plates between the head and the tail. Keep the meat clustered together and let the tomato sauce run all over the plate. Tell your friends that this is an Mongolian delicacy.

If you want have some real fun with this recipe, don't offer any forks- make them use chopsticks. Not that using chopsticks has any special meaning, it's just fun to watch people eat with chopsticks.

Slob Kebabs

Complexity rating- 5

Needed (serves 4):
2 dozen clams
2 dozen mussels
1 package of crabmeat chunks
1 clove of garlic
1 dozen tiny onions
1 green pepper
8 cherry tomatoes
1 lb. of stew meat chunks
1 cup of teriyaki sauce
4 skewers

-Steam clams, mussels, and garlic in frying pan with butter to firm up the clams and mussels while softening the garlic

-When finished, place the stew meat in the pan and braise

-While meat braises, chop peppers into 2 inch squares.

-Put all ingredients on the skewers

-Pour teriyaki generously over everything

-Place skewers on grill for several minutes until cooked

It may look nasty, but it tastes delicious!!!

To add a little challenge, be sure to "accidentally" forget any silverware or plates.

Glossary

Aft- Anything behind you on a boat

Anchor- A boater's nickname for a spouse (see also Ball and Chain)

Ballast- Secret nickname given to any fat person who boards your boat

Binding Post- a post that, when eaten, immediately solidifies all BM's

Boat Hook- phenomenon of becoming addicted to boating

Bow- What seasick passengers do over the rail.

Cradle- Where you would like to curl up after a brutal day of boating

Dingy- Something your wife utilizes while you are traveling on business

Draft- Beer that is poured from a tap in the boat club.

Engine Block- Something that your engine sits on for months while you attempt to repair it.

Head- 1) A room on a boat in which all major decisions are made. 2) Captains quarters

Isolators- extremely ugly boaters who do not associate with mainstream boaters

Manifold- What you say after having been dealt a lousy hand while having a poker game on the boat ("man, I fold").

Motor- The non-working block of iron that sits on the stern of most boats

Nautical- A retail term that, when added to any object, increases the cost of that object by forty percent

Port- A type of wine served on deck after dinner

Rope- What you call a line when no other boaters are there to judge you

Salty Dog- A low grade, high sodium frankfurter frequently eaten by boaters

Slip- What happens when you walk on deck in your socks.

Stern- The look you receive from your spouse when you start talking about upgrading.

Strut- What you do immediately following the purchase of a new boat.

Teak- A type of wood from India that is very resistant to rot but dulls if you stick your tongue out at it.

Thru-Hull- Where logs wind up when you hit them at speed

Waterproof- Fictitious term which implies that it is possible to keep something (anything) dry

Windlass- The name given to the spouse that usually pulls the anchor

Top Ten Reasons
to Sell A Boat

1. You have completely forgotten your spouse and children's names.

2. That 1/2 inch line just keeps getting heavier and heavier.

3. You just watched "A Perfect Storm."

4. You keep forgetting to put that damned plug in.

5. Your kid can now back it into the slip better than you.

6. Lately, you've been finding the allure of crochet simply irresistible.

7. Your backyard is beginning to look like a tropical rain forest.

8. You've developed a phobia against spiders.

9. Your barnacles come up over the side and join you for morning coffee.

10. Upgrade!!

ORDER FORM

To order additional copies of *What's a Hoy?*
complete and send the order form below

Order Form
What's a Hoy? A Guide to Modern Boating

Name_____

Street Address_____

State_____ Zip_____

Daytime Phone_____

Quantity	Price	Total
_____	x 14.95 =	_____

add shipping $2.00 each   _____
add 7% sales tax   _____
Total   _____

Make checks payable to Argo Press

Mail to:
Argo Press, Inc.
P.O. Box 655
Shrub Oak, NY 10588

* If you are sending this book to someone as a gift, please also complete the form on the next page.

Send To:

Name_____

Street Address_____

State_____ Zip_____

Please Check All That Apply

Dear_____,

- ❏ Congratulations on buying your new boat
- ❏ Congratulations on selling your boat
- ❏ Congratulations on your marriage
- ❏ Congratulations on your divorce
- ❏ I have been on your boat and have seen your seamanship first hand- this book might help
- ❏ I have experienced your interpersonal skills- this book might help
- ❏ You seem to really need a good laugh
- ❏ This book takes the place of the money I owe you
- ❏ I was reminded of you on page _____
- ❏ I am and always have been a more skilled boater than you
- ❏ I give this to clients rather than friends to get a tax deduction
- ❏ At least you know more about boating than the guy who wrote this book
- ❏ _____
  _____
  _____
  _____

Sincerely,

_____

133

ANOTHER ORDER FORM

In case you've already used the other order form and still wish to order additional copies of *What's a Hoy?* complete and send the order form below

Order Form
What's a Hoy? A Guide to Modern Boating

Name_____

Street Address_____

State_____ Zip_____

Daytime Phone_____

Quantity   Price   Total
_____ x   14.95   =   _____

add shipping $2.00   _____
add 7% sales tax   _____
Total   _____

Make checks payable to Argo Press

Mail to:
Argo Press, Inc.
P.O. Box 655
Shrub Oak, NY 10588

* If you are sending this book to someone as a gift, please also complete the form on the next page.

Send To:

Name_____

Street Address_____

State_____ Zip_____

Please Check All That Apply

Dear_____,

- ❏ Congratulations on buying your new boat
- ❏ Congratulations on selling your boat
- ❏ Congratulations on your marriage
- ❏ Congratulations on your divorce
- ❏ I have been on your boat and have seen your seamanship first hand- this book might help
- ❏ I have experienced your interpersonal skills- this book might help
- ❏ You seem to really need a good laugh
- ❏ This book takes the place of the money I owe you
- ❏ I was reminded of you on page _____
- ❏ I am and always have been a more skilled boater than you
- ❏ I give this to clients rather than friends to get a tax deduction
- ❏ At least you know more about boating than the guy who wrote this book
- ❏ _____
_____
_____
_____

Sincerely,

_____

137

About the Author

Cap'n Drew Brown was born in Brooklyn and raised in Rockaway Beach, Queens.

He bought his first boat in 1990 and began immediately running aground in the Hudson River where he does the majority of his boating. Always pushing farther and further, he ventured on to other, more distant waterways where he could run aground on new shoals. His boating accomplishments include a trip with his wife in his twenty-six footer up to the Maine coast from New York using no electronic navigation equipment. The following year they went south (also "Christopher Columbus style"). He prides himself in the fact that he has run aground in nine states.

He Lives in Westchester County NY with his wife Meg (Windlass) and his three children- son Fender, daughter Cleat and 26 foot Bayliner, Carpe Diem. He writes a monthly humor column **Ask Cap'n Drew** that appears monthly in *Boating on the Hudson* and *The Fishin' For 'Um Magazines*.